Community
Landscape Design

Design Media Publishing Limited

Contents

Preface

As the world is undergoing rapid urbanisation and demands for good housing in cities soar, we are looking for residential environments where we can take refuge from our intense and hectic lifestyle. This enticing book is a window to diverse range of community landscape design creating exceptional living environments across the globe addressing this need of high-quality housing. Filled with exciting images from projects designed by renowned international firms this book is a visual treat for all professionals, students and design lovers. Showcasing ways to choreograph unique experiences in residential developments it gives us a comprehensive portrait of inspiring landscape projects worldwide. This stimulating book is divided broadly into three sections – high-rise residential tower landscape, mid-rise residential block landscape and the low-rise villa landscape as each category has its unique landscape character. The high-rise residential blocks are increasingly integrating vertical green features as part of façade with sky decks and terrace gardens. Open spaces incorporating all the community facilities are generally on decks with parking below. In contrast, the landscape feel in mid-rise residential block developments is more of being in a courtyard environment. Very often roof gardens become another space for community interaction in this form of development as allotment gardens and urban farms. The landscape design for villa development with its low-rise architecture has its own intimate feel and character. With private gardens, leafy streets and community greens it is a delicate interplay of finer texture and scale evoking its unique charm and sense of place. Bringing all these disparate design approaches together under one comprehensive volume makes this book a stimulating and inspiring journey through the world of contemporary residential landscape.

Landscape design for residential developments is becoming increasingly diverse in its scale and ambition. Due to advancement of technology and blurring of work-life boundary, our home as a refuge is increasingly becoming crucial in fostering our well being. Hence designers are moving towards creating oasis like spaces where residential developments are conceived with lavish pools and extensive gardens. As a result, new outdoor experiences integrating art and culture are staring to evolve as the boundary between indoor and outdoor spaces blur. Landscape design is unique in many senses. The key tool for creating spaces remains the use of plants that grows and changes with time. The dynamic plant cycle with its colour and texture mixed with hardscape elements give landscape architects a vibrant set of materials to play with. Water with its various forms adds fluidity and reflection as well as calmness and movement. Lighting at night adds its own drama. Equipped with these tools landscape architects can create a unique and dramatic experiences in projects where culture, context, sustainability and budget form some of the key parameters.

The beautifully articulated projects in the book demonstrate how landscape architects integrate these parameters in their projects. For example, Shma's SUMMER project near Bangkok is a stunning choreography of art, architecture and nature. It is a landscape where context of sea is abstracted in a series of unique geometrical forms to create a dramatic experience. Linking culture and context in abstract form is demonstrated in the sublime design of Trop's Baan Sansuk development. Here the interplay between rocks and boulders with water create a grand setting for the residential courtyard. Another project that beautifully integrates the context of water in its physicality is Rolfsbukta in Oslo, Norway by Bjorbekk and Lindhelm where water is brought into the site through a canal connected to the bay. Sustainability plays a dominant role and becomes a big driver for projects like The Neo Bankside in London by Gillespies and Block 32 at Rino, Denver by studioINSITE. Both the projects generate unique character by using native planting and fostering local biodiversity. In Block 32 the installations integrated with solar panels as sculptural elements no doubt form a playful response to the project's location within the art district.

Creating compelling public spaces with limited budget for social housing projects is always a challenge. However projects like Exemplary Social Housing Project in Munich by Irene Burkhart Landscape Architects and 209 Guadabajaque Council Housing in Jerez de la Frontera, Spain by Acta Sim, Manuel Narvaez Perez and Fernando Visedo Manzanares show how simple and sensitive approach to design can create great community landscape for residents to enjoy. Inclusion of exemplary social housing landscape projects in this book is no coincidence as large population migrates to cities and look for affordable housing. Undoubtedly social housing landscape will be one of the key areas for future landscape design.Another new avenue of residential design will stem from the aging population. A design that is sensitive, imaginative and community focused will be the key in fulfilling user aspiration. Designers need to consider the aspects of safety, materiality and accessibility to generate a holistic living environment for the elderly.

In order to address global environmental issues as more regulation and certification will be required, landscape design as a whole will also evolve accordingly. One example will be the extensive use of roof gardens – spaces for both gardening and farming. We will increasingly see building façades, especially in high-rise buildings with more green walls in form of vertical greening. In a dense urban condition the roof gardens along with the green façades will evolve as elevated ecological network integrating landscape, architecture, art and engineering. As new ideas emerge and how we design community spaces evolve, our role as landscape architects will become more important than ever.

So watch the space!

Viraj Chatterjee

B Arch (Hons), MLA (Distinction),
CMLI, MCA, AIIA
Founder and Design Principal, ONE landscape
Assistant Professor of Landscape Architecture, Hong Kong University

• *Mid-rise residential block landscape*

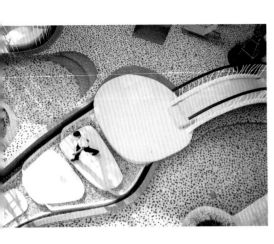

SUMMER

Location: Bangkok, Thailand
Completion: 2013
Design: Shma Company Limited
Photography: Mr. Pirak Anurakyawachon
Area: 9,982 sqm

The project is located at famous seaside town called Hua Hin which is situated about 300 km south of Bangkok. The site is in irregular shape of approximately 9,982 square metres. The main landscape area is surrounded by an L shape building where it leaves the other 2 sides visually connected with the nearby private garden. Since the site is situated far away from the beach and half of the residential units cannot receive sea view, the landscape design strategy is to create landscape that not only functions as an outdoor hideaway space but also reflects "Seascape" atmosphere as the residents would feel closer to the sea.

In other words, the design concept derives from the "sea bubble" which occurs once the wave roll over the shores. The bubbles come in various size and none of them are looking the same. The designers conceptually use the bubble form to generate the overall design. The landscape space is divided into two: swimming pool and garden. The pool is located at the higher level next to the building while garden is next to the wall next to private villas. The large water body of the pool covers 50% of the landscape area and spans across the whole length of building edge, providing a direct pool access of all ground floor units. It also contains various water related activities within this surface from 25 m lap pool, children pool, shallow pool, submerge pool deck with bubble water jet and Jacuzzi, to sunken cabana. With this unique curved shape of pool edge, it provides not only the ultimate setting for each activities but also a better functioning space for garden level which is lowered by 450 mm. The overflowing water at the pool edge creates a tranquil fluid sound ambience for the whole landscape area. At the garden, bubble shape becomes a primary form in generating spaces which composed of stepping

Master plan

stone, planters, lawn, gravel beds and cabanas.

There are 3 cabanas in cylindrical shape range in various heights from 4 to 5 metres which are nicely placed between the pool curvatures and become main focal points from all directions. One of the cabana is the pavilion to provide certain privacy for Jacuzzi zone while the other 2 are daybed and seating area which are only accessible from the garden level. The shape of the cabana and the pattern of the trellis are also inspired from "Sea Wave". A series of 30 mm diameter of linear tubes were bended to create curve lines at difference heights. As a result, the subtle rhythm of cabana shells exposes a unique light and shadow play. With its forms and white

coloured structure of Trellis, it contrasts with dark green backdrop of the garden behind so it emphasises itself as a sculpture during the day and lanterns at night, with series of up lights that were integrated at each steel tubes.

The colour palette of hard-scape and soft-cape elements here is in neutral and light pastel colour composition. It is to create a calm and serene atmosphere for this hideaway place while giving a wide open feeling to the overall space.

This landscape space is the designer's interpretation of the "Seascape" for the hideaway of modern living.

1. The garden next to the swimming pool
2. The large water body of the pool covers 50% of the landscape area

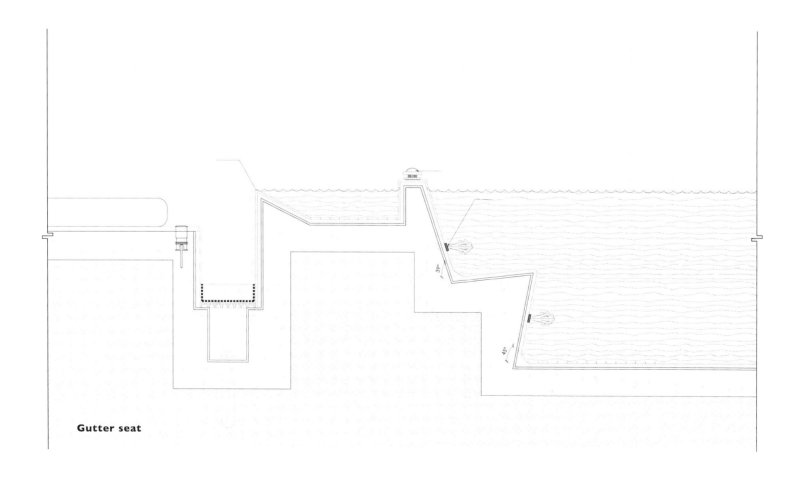

Gutter seat

3. A small bridge across the pool
4. Cabanas in cylindrical shape
5. The seating

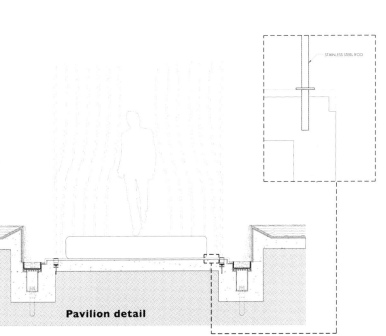

STAINLESS STEEL ROD

Pavilion detail

6~8. The paving in the garden
9. Lush green plants growing along the path
10. Bird eye view at night
11. Stepping stone and gravel beds

10

11

SARI BY SANSIRI

Location: Bangkok, Thailand
Completion: 2013
Design: Shma Company Limited
Design Director: Yossapon Boonsom
Landscape Architect: Ken Chongsuwat,
Ponlawat Pootai
Photography: Mr.Pirak Anurakyawachon
Area: 1,062.41sqm

Water is necessary to all life, the landscape expresses this essence of nature through architecture and applies the design in the form of "River Delta". With a limited accommodation area for 7-floors residents, the landscape becomes most essential for its people. The project is divided into East and West buildings, leaving a gap in between to receive enough winds for all rooms. River Delta is then translated into landscape architecture and takes part in uniting the overall into one.

Characters of river are expressed richly in bold graphics of architectural environments, from finishing to spatial space. Natural elements of trees, bushes, gravels and woods are finely arranged to create an easeful environment in rigid geometrical forms. On rooftop garden, entrance ground is shifted down to connect with lower fitness floor, planters are raised to create a zigzag river walk boundary, and extended pocket space of grass lawn brings panoramic viewing experience to visitors.

The landscape is divided into 2 functioning areas on each roof garden. East building occupies by strolling area and resting area on the opposite side which both connect to lap pools that extend along the west edge. West building is for a more private couch surrounded by greenery and BBQ lawn facing east, which has a sunken walkway in between. The two sides that facing each other, are visually connected with transparent glass railing while all the rest are solid walls either are tall bush or concrete railing.

An alignment of finished materials are placed accordingly from east to west, connecting all landscape areas together. Dynamic patterns of vertical fins turn machine room into another curious volume yet camouflage soundly as part of landscape elements. The finished wall turns into an elusive light and shadow play at night, and provides shade for the pool during the day. Bush planters at the river walk slope up to wrap resting area with greenery. Trees are planted above private couch and daybed by the pool, becoming green lush scenery for both sides. At ground floor, double-height ceiling entrance finished with warmth wood texture expresses formality, in contrast to the rooftop garden.

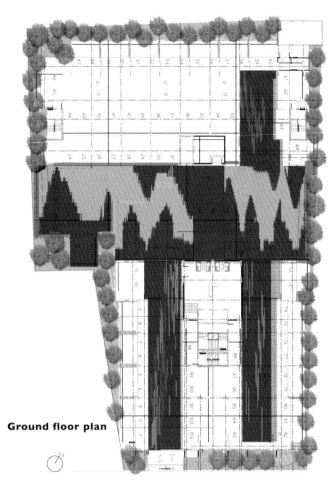

Ground floor plan

Ultimately, design that accommodates greenery could drive growth of urban ecology along with the city's economic environment. It not only creates positive impact such as reducing heat which is crucial to tropical city, but also encourages outdoor activities for public health and importantly mitigates negative impacts to the urban environment.

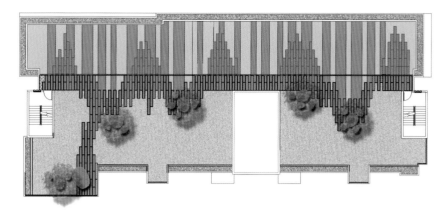

Roof floor plan

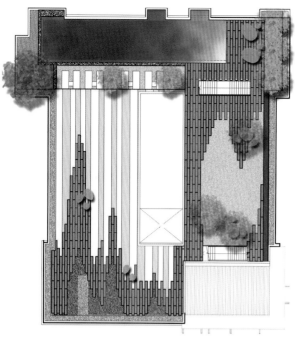

Roof floor plan

1. Façade view
2. Bird eye view
3. The roof garden

4. Strolling area
5. Lap pools
6. Resting area

Custom seat

7-9. Details of the grass lawn and gravels
10. Night view of the pool
11. Night view of the strolling area

10

11

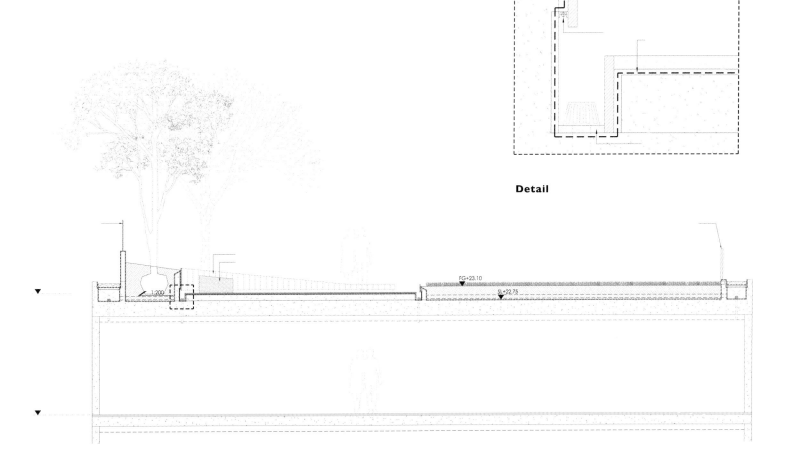

Detail

FG+23.10

SL+22.75

1:200

BAAN SANSUK

Location: Hua-Hin, Thailand
Design: TROP
Photography: Pattarapol Jormkhanngen, Pok Kobkongsanti
Area: 11,613sqm

Baan Sansuk is an exclusive residential project, located at Hua Hin, Thailand's favourite Beach. The impressive nature style condominium contains a 230-metre-long modern seascape swimming pool, which provides amusement for kids and the peaceful dreamy relaxing days for adults. Baan Sansuk is situated in the prime-location of Hua Hin beach, only a few minutes to Chatchai Market and all other conveniences.

The site is long, noodle-like with a small narrow side connected to the beach. There are 2 rows of buildings on both sides, leaving a long space in the middle of the site. Basically, most of the units, except the beach-front ones, do not have any ocean view. Instead they are facing the opposite units.

The designers' first move is to bring "the view" into the property instead. Their inspiration of "the view" comes from the location of the project. Hua Hin, in Thai, means Stone Head. The name comes from the natural stone boulders in its beach area. So the designers proposed a series of swimming pools from the lobby to the beach area, a total of 230 m long.

The Pools are divided into several types, with different functions like Reflecting Pool, Kids Pool, Transitional Pool, Jacuzzi Pool and Main Pool. At some certain area, the designers strategically place Natural Stone Boulders to mimic the Famed Local Beach. The result is a breath-taking Water Landscape, with different Water Characters from one end of the site to the other. These pools are not just for eye-pleasure only, but they also serve as the pools for everyone in the family.

The site plan

1. Landscape lighting in front of the building
2-3. The site is a long, noodle-like with a small narrow side connected to the beach
4. Water landscape

5-6. The swimming pool
7 The designers strategically place Natural Stone Boulders to mimic the Famed Local Beach at some certain area
8-9. Bird eye view of the pools

BAAN SAN KRAAM

Location: Cha-Am, Petchaburi, Thailand
Completion: 2013
Design: Sanitas Studio Co., Ltd.
Photography: Wison Tungthunya
Area: 23,110sqm

Sanitas Studio was commissioned in 2011 by Sansiri PLC to devise a masterplan and landscape design for Baan San Kraam, a residential project on Cha-Am beach, Petchaburi, Thailand. Only 10 per cent of its extensive area borders the beach meaning just two of the thirteen buildings have a direct sea view. The challenge for Sanitas was to provide a landscape design allowing all residents to feel equally close to the beach.

Starting with a nautical nostalgia theme, Sanitas envisaged the land as an abstract form of the ocean. It would contain different elements of islands and seascape such as jungle, villages and a floating house. Seven clusters of buildings were then created with their own unique seascape character.

The landscape design is a simple interpretation of the wave typology. Having studied its form in detail, Sanitas has developed it into three-dimensional landscape form. This includes wave seating, stepping stones, rock day beds and a tree house, while water is the landscape's key element and connects all zones together.

Residents can experience the different character of each area from their arrival at Lobby Beach and then across the water to the Jungle which is surrounded by secluded villages. Local coastal plants enhance the natural beauty of the development and its stunning oceanside concept, while existing trees have been preserved to provide welcome shaded area.

"Ocean" Concept

Starting with nautical nostalgia, Sanitas Studio envisages the land as an abstract form of the ocean. The abstract ocean would contain different characters of islands and seascape: the jungle, the villages, the floating house and the sea tide. This would create different atmosphere for each cluster of buildings. Then the designers create seven clusters of building with their own unique seascape character, from Lobby Beach, Fisherman Village, Modern Jungle, Village Tree House, Village Pool, Connecting Beach and Floating House.

Master plan

Wave Typology

From the "ocean" concept, the water body is the key landscape element, which connects all zones together. The designers studied the natural form of the seascape and interpret it in modern way. In the overall masterplan, the form of landscape is a simplification of topography line of the ocean and uses it as the landscape language throughout the whole site.

The landscape design is a simple interpretation of the wave typology. Sanitas Studio studied the form of sea wave and developed it in the landscape form three dimensionally. It becomes part of the continuous seating, continuous steps, the retaining wall and planters.

Site Layout

At Baan San Kraam, the "ocean" concept plays an important role and connects all zones together with one unique landscape language of seascape. The water body, where all activities are met, is associated with pathway system and sunbathing deck and is partially adjacent to the balconies of some units, so people can connect to the swimming pool directly.

At Baan San Kraam, Sanitas Studio has created a series of rich details for each zone, which become its own internal view and provide a series of outdoor sitting areas, so people can enjoy resting in each unique garden. From the front entrance, the residents could arrive on the Lobby Beach with horizontal line of beachscape, across the water to the Jungle with rustic plants which is surrounded by secluded villages. There is a sunken island for Gym room, so people can exercise with a view of water cascade and have sun-bathing on the roof deck. Before arriving on the beach, there was a large swimming pool and sunbathing terraces.

At Baan San Kraam, soft planting also plays an important role; nurturing the space, differentiating characteristic of each zone, providing shade for outdoor function space and decreasing temperature, which is crucial in tropical country. The existing trees have a big impact on landscape's atmosphere, especially for each front area, where there are stunningly mature Rain tree, Flame tree and Tamarind tree.

Circulation

At Baan San Kraam, there is a vehicle access from the street with front parking under trellis structure. After arrival at the lobby, people can choose to walk through the main walkway, which connects to all buildings or choose the golf cart-service and access from the service way, which runs along the periphery. The parking is located at the entrance area and provides service for mechanical room and garbage room.

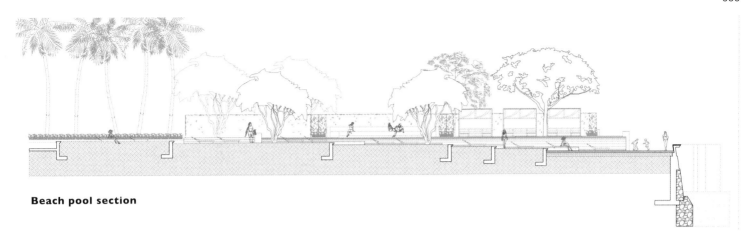

Beach pool section

1. The designer envisaged the land as an abstract form of the ocean.
2. The "ocean" concept plays an important role

3. Outdoor sitting area
4. The white paving among the green plants
5. Sunbathing terrace
6. Sunken island for Gym room at night

Gym section

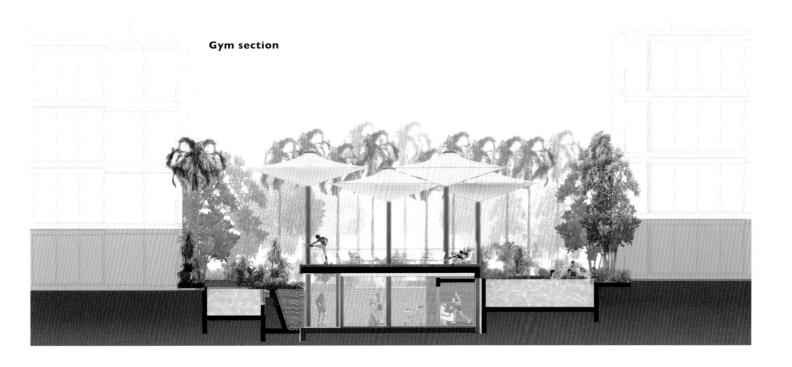

7. Unique seascape character
8-10. A series of rich details
11. Sunken island for Gym room in daylight

NEO BANKSIDE

Location: London, UK
Completion: 2013
Design: Gillespies
Photography: Jason Gairn
Area: 7,700sqm

Developed as an integral part of the residential scheme, the new landscapes at NEO Bankside provide richly-detailed green areas that balance beautifully with the contemporary apartment pavilions. Unusually in the heart of the city, the new outdoor spaces offer NEO Bankside's residents unique opportunities to engage with nature.

The landscape designs take cues from natural processes found within woodlands, and transpose them to the city. A beehive is installed, and an orchard of fruiting trees and an herb garden give residents access to produce, and add colour and fragrance to the garden areas.

As with any residential development located in the heart of a city, outdoor space was restricted, but Gillespies' designs sought to ensure that NEO Bankside's exterior spaces reached their full potential.

NEO Bankside's green spaces offer both residents and members of the public passing through a mix of the landscape typologies we find in nature. This approach creates a rich microcosm of landscapes within a constrained footprint.

Sustainability and Environmental Considerations

Gillespies' designers placed great importance on selecting the most appropriate materials for NEO Bankside's landscapes in respect to the environment, place-making and long-term performance. Gillespies specified all elements as suitable for the context, to limit impact on the environment, and where relevant, to be robust and tolerant enough for the stresses of a public environment over a long period of time.

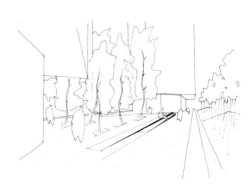

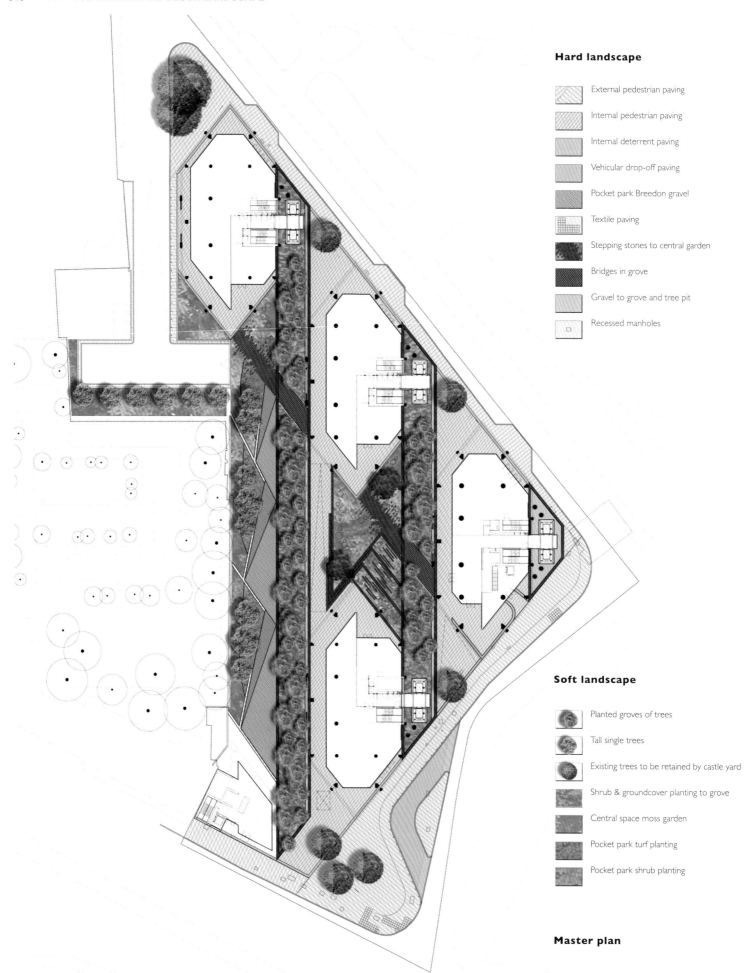

Hard landscape

External pedestrian paving

Internal pedestrian paving

Internal deterrent paving

Vehicular drop-off paving

Pocket park Breedon gravel

Textile paving

Stepping stones to central garden

Bridges in grove

Gravel to grove and tree pit

Recessed manholes

Soft landscape

Planted groves of trees

Tall single trees

Existing trees to be retained by castle yard

Shrub & groundcover planting to grove

Central space moss garden

Pocket park turf planting

Pocket park shrub planting

Master plan

Working with planting specialists Growth Industry, Gillespies included large tracts of native plants into the design, set within groves of trees to provide a "bank" of flowers, seeds and nesting material to encourage biodiversity and a range of wildlife to the space.

1. The new landscapes provide richly-detailed green areas that balance beautifully with the contemporary apartment pavilions
2-3. The green spaces offer both residents and members of the public passing through a mix of the landscape typologies we find in nature

4. Bird eye view of the overall landscape
5. The detail of the paving
6. The side view of the sculpture
7. The detail of the flower bed
8. The planting softens the built environment
9-11. A "bank" of flowers

Rainwater Harvesting for Irrigation

Working with Hoare Lea engineers, the scheme evolved to ensure capacity for rainwater harvesting was a central tenet of the basement design and construction. Water retention boards (reservoirs) were laid over the structural slab – this technology provides a reserve of water to maintain soil saturation and consequently limits the amount of irrigation water required. This reserve of water supplements the planting irrigation system, and limits the demands on mains water use.

Planting and Biodiversity

The planting concepts and final details are central to the overall landscape design for NEO Bankside. The planting softens the built environment, humanises the space and mitigates the local microclimate to create comfortable, welcoming spaces. It also provides a seasonal sense of time and place to enrich urban life. Most of the plants used at NEO Bankside are native in origin and are carefully suited to the microclimate of the site. BREEAM guidelines and biodiversity were major drivers for the selection of appropriate plant species.

BLOCK 32 AT RINO

Location: Denver, USA
Completion: 2013
Design: studioINSITE
Photography: studioINSITE
Area: 16,187sqm
Awards: 2013 Denver Mayor's Design Award, 2013 Denver Multifamily Project of the Year, awarded by the Rocky Mountain Real Estate Expo

The Block 32 at RiNo project offers two hundred and five multi-family rental housing units within the burgeoning RiverNorth (RiNo) District just blocks north of downtown Denver, Colorado. The space is designed to celebrate the unique urban character of the up-and-coming RiNo Art District, with its high concentration of creative businesses and array of studio spaces in an industrial environment. studioINSITE provided site design and landscape architecture to the client for the four acre site.

The Block 32 development has been designed with the flexibility for potential ground-level commercial space, allowing for a live-work community. Block 32 at RiNo is constructed around a shared courtyard that offers a space for continued community interaction. With space for both active and passive use around planted areas, a swimming pool and spa, the Block 32 courtyard remains an active amenity zone. Residents enjoy the outdoor patios, completed with outdoor televisions, speakers, barbeques, foosball, ping-pong and even a bocce ball court.

The building's bold colours of red and yellow are echoed in the playful red site furniture. Plantings at the site include native grasses, bamboo, yucca and bright blooming annuals. The selected trees include Thornless Cockspur Hawthorn, Autumn Brilliance Serviceberry, Japanese Tree Lilac, and Chanticleer Pear. The design uses industrial materials in unusual ways to solve a variety of functional issues while reinforcing the "artistic" characteristics of the project. Playful shapes can be found throughout; the swimming pool and topographical courtyard landscape forms take on organic and unexpected shapes.

Sustainable features are a prominent part of the project. The complex is designed to meet Enterprise Green Community standards. Highly visible along Brighton Boulevard, a solar panel trellis is one of the focal points of the project. It showcases the use of renewable energy while also providing shade. Due to urban storm

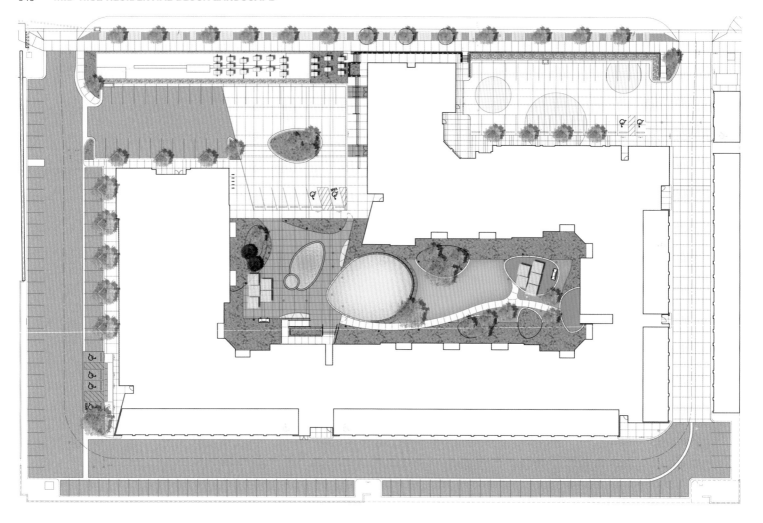

Master plan

1. The shared courtyard landscape
2. Elliptical green lawn
3. The Block 32 courtyard remains an active amenity zone

water drainage concerns, studioINSITE incorporated a state-of-the-art detention facility into the landscape architecture for the property, using an imaginative wall to integrate it with the character of the neighbourhood.

Helping to transform the face of the RiverNorth district, Block 32 at RiNohas earned recognition as part of an "area of change" in the Denver Metropolitan Area. The project has won two awards: the 2013 Denver Mayor's Design Award, and the 2013 Denver Multifamily Project of the Year, awarded by the Rocky Mountain Real Estate Expo.

4. The building's bold colours of red and yellow are echoed in the playful red site furniture
5-6. Details of the swimming pool
7-9. Plantings at the site include native grasses, bamboo, yucca and bright blooming annuals

ROLFSBUKTA

Location: Oslo, Norway
Design: Bjørbekk & Lindheim AS
Architect: ARCASA architects, Norway
Photography: Bjørbekk & Lindheim AS
Area: 66,000sqm

Rolfsbukta is a bay at the north-east end of Fornebu. It is one of the few points where residential areas on the site of the old airport will have direct contact with the sea.

Very early in the project a decision was reached to reinforce the relationship of the bay with the sea and consequently a canal was extended into the bay. To bring the water as close as possible to the public, the landscape designer planned the inner 2/3 of the canal as a freshwater canal and the last 1/3 as a deep saltwater canal, connected by a waterfall between the two levels.

The residential area, Pollen, surrounding the inner part of the fresh water canal, is already completed. A large pool, a pond with stepping stones, a wooden pier and a fountain frame two sides of the Pollen buildings. The water surface is enclosed by a poured concrete ramp that slopes down on one side, and on the other sides stairs lead down to a 20 centimetre deep pool. The canal is surrounded by formal beds of ornamental grasses and willow trees framed by non-corrosive steel, the same material as is used in a custom-made barbecue. There are several seats surrounding the pool made of poured concrete with wooden covering recessed into the concrete. There is also a large platform of trees planted in gravel together with long tables and benches.

The seating, the "island" and the bridge are lit from below creating the impression that they are floating as the dark falls. More lighting is directed up towards the trees from the planter boxes, throughout the platforms, on the "island" and at the base of the spray nozzles of the water fountain. Various species of willows and cherry trees are planted close to the canal together with the ornamental grasses Chinese Silver Grass, Purple Moor Grass and Silver Feather Grass.

Further out at Rolfsbukta the second part of Phase 1, Tangen and Marina, have been completed. The pier motif with promenade is an essential part of this housing

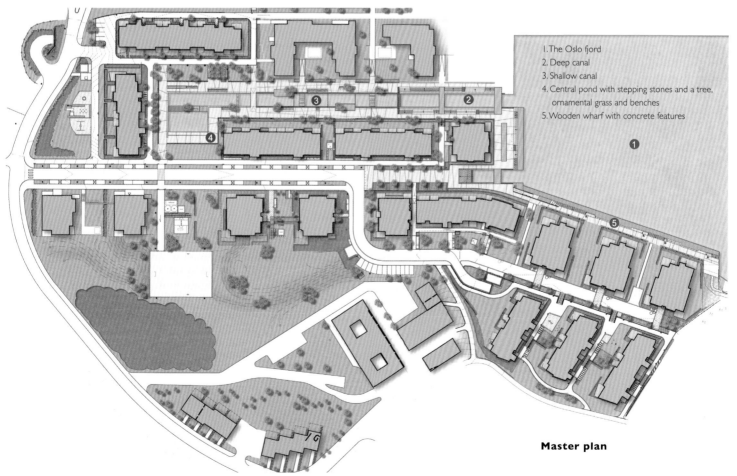

1. The Oslo fjord
2. Deep canal
3. Shallow canal
4. Central pond with stepping stones and a tree, ornamental grass and benches
5. Wooden wharf with concrete features

Master plan

complex that is made up of 6 blocks on a north-west facing slope down towards the sea. You can moor boats and walk out along the bay to the outmost tip of the bay. This sunny west-facing waterfront is designed for recreation. Poured concrete embankments provide steps and seating.

Ground-floor front gardens have a garden raised by about 80 cm and planted with a screen of vegetation to protect privacy. Within the Marina there is a car-free, green, spacious residential street with stairs to the upper residential area, Tangen. Custom made granite stones engraved with the addresses on each level offer a place to sit down and also demarcate each entrance.

Paths between the blocks provide good access to the sea also for those who live in the back rows. Because views of the sea and sun are meaningful, small trees, such as magnolia, Japanese Judas-trees, cherry and rowan trees have been chosen. Alpine currant bushes, beech, purple osier willows, virginia creeper, lilac, waxberries, black chokeberries, juneberries and common ivy are other plant types to be found in the area.

1. The residential area surrounds the inner part of the fresh water
2. A car-free spacious residential street
3. Stepping stones
4. Water fountain
5. The pond-area with stepping stones, a wooden "island", a water fountain, surrounded by formal beds of ornamental grasses, willow trees and concrete benches

6. The sunny north-west facing bench is designed for recreation
7. Benches of poured concrete with wooden covering surrounds the pond-area
8. Extensive use of corten steel in the details
9. Ornamental grass
10. Silver feather grass, stipa calamagrostis

8

9

10

MODE 61

Location: Bangkok, Thailand
Design: Shma Company Limited
Photography: Pirak Anurakyawachon
Area: 3,200sqm

In response to dense urban surroundings of Bangkok, the main landscape area is conceived as an internal courtyard to create an inverted tranquility with all surrounding units looking into garden spaces. The landscape space is split in multi-level to achieve privacy between garden space and the units within limited space and also to create a dynamic view from the balcony looking down. This is resulted in three-dimensional plays of water and greenery; from reflective pond to water wall, from green roof to green wall.

At entrance, a relationship with public was taken into consideration. Rather than having a solid surface at the front boundary wall, a row of green hedge at 1.8-meter-high coupled with another layer of bamboo aligned behind it standing up to 6 meters high is incorporated to form a boundary. A natural environment from these layers of green is given not only to act as a soft screen for residential units facing to the main street but also to fulfill a public realm by adding greenery to this relatively dry neighborhood.

By entering to drop-off area, one faces with warm feature wooden wall protecting private area from exposure to chaotic pedestrians. The threshold lead people to enter from the side and while they are approaching lobby, a delicate white sculpture stands before their eyes with layers of green and water body as a background. The alfresco lobby is designed to locate under green roof which helps to absorb tropical heat and to be surrounded by cascade water which provides passive cooling without air-conditioner to reduce electrical power consumptions.

From lobby to the signature swimming pool area, wooden steps accompanied with overflow cascade by the side lead people to escalate up infusing into another space. The level of pool deck is carefully determined to elevate slightly from the lobby and to drop by 2 meters from the units on the first floor to give a sense of privacy for each areas. Changing of levels is crafted with water wall and green wall creating a tranquil ambience as a backdrop for the pool area. Willow is selected as a feature tree to envelop the pool space for its feather light leaf draping down

1. Overview

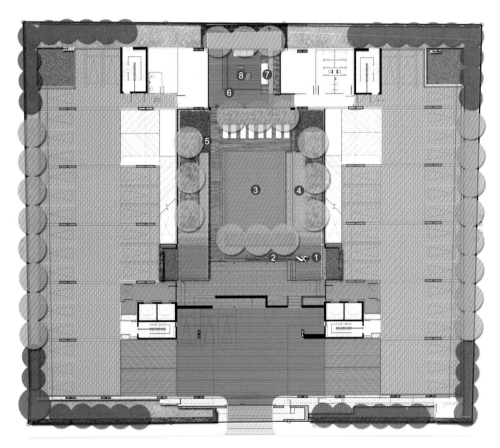

1. Sculpture
2. Timber bench
3. Swimming pool
4. Water wall
5. Green wall
6. Sunken lounge
7. Sofa
8. Timber table

Master plan

2. Sunken lounge
3. Sunken lounge with built-in sofa

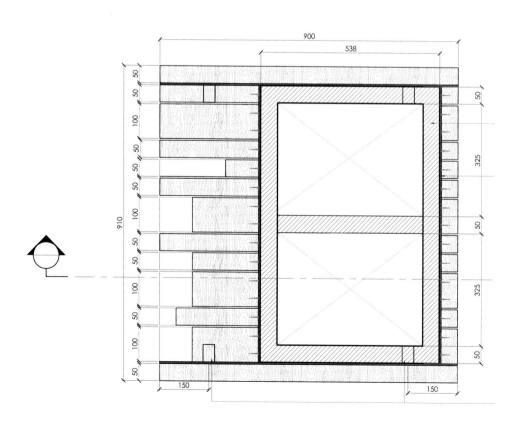

Timber table sectional plan

3

forming a natural blind for the privacy of the room and swimming pool.

Consequently, moving through the pool deck to the sunken lounge where built-in reclining sofa enclaves amongst plantations. The space is designed to serve family lounging or even small party/gathering in the garden setting next to the reading room. When needed, sliding glass door of the reading room can be fully open connecting to the sunken lounge space forming a larger function spaces. The stone paving material extends horizontally to the adjacent reading room to emphasize a continuum of outdoor and indoor spaces.

The landscape of Mode 61 is created as a private green nest instilling a contemplative living environment throughunderstated space composition and meticulous detailing. Altogether, surfaces finished in a well-defined natural stone and enriched with intricate detailing of wood work from the entrance wall to outdoor lounges, bring about an urban yet rustic outdoor dwelling. Ultimately, all meticulous detailing is curated modernly yet bio-mimicking contemplative composition.

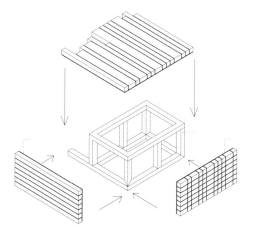

Feature Plants

Large Tree
- Salix babylonica Linn
- Indian Oak
- Bamboo
- Indian Cork Tree
- Mahogany

Small Plants
- Iris
- Ophiopogon japonicus (Kyoto Dwarf)
- Dwarf Umbrella Tree
- Spike Moss Family
- Alocasia Indica (Elephant Ear)
- Bromeliad
- Succulent

4. The plantings
5. Paving material extends from the sunken lounge to the adjacent reading room
6. Delicate white sculpture and timber bench

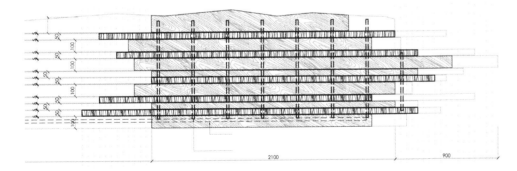

Timber bench plan

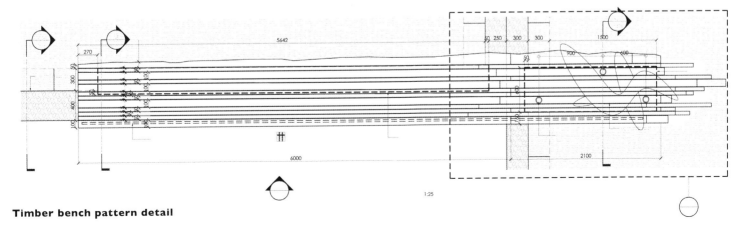

1:25

Timber bench pattern detail

RENOVATION OF OUTDOOR AREAS BISPEHAVEN HOUSING ESTATE

Location: Aarhus, Denmark
Design: Vibeke Rønnow Landskabsarkitekter,
C. F. Møller Architects
Photography: Helene Hoyer Mikkelsen
Area: 170,000sqm

The outdoor areas around the Bispehaven social housing estate, built in 1970, were characterised by extensive surfaced areas, high concrete walls and dense planting, producing a dull and insecure environment.

Despite the attractive flats and the near-town location, the area had acquired the reputation of being something of a ghetto, with much vandalism and difficulty in attracting tenants. The aim of the total renovation project has been to give the area a new identity and quality, in particular by creating new meeting-places for the residents.

The outdoor areas have been given a sense of openness and simplicity by replacing the dense planting with lawns and flower beds. The distinctive slopes surrounding the development have been cleared of scrub and have become open grassy surfaces with sculptural rows of birch trees. The former high concrete walls have been sawn of near ground level, to become low balustrades.

The new paving uses a restrained palette of black and white patterns, to match the renovated facades of the housing scheme, and the plantings are equally kept simple with mainly wisteria, privet, various grasses and slender Himalayan birch trees.

The sloping terrain has been made use of to provide sitting steps, and residents can take part in activities on multi-functional squares and spaces, which include a covered stage and special areas for dancing, skating and ball games. Four footbridges provide new icons for the area. Together with new, more secure lighting, they also help to provide landmarks in the night, each illuminated in its own colour.

Master plan

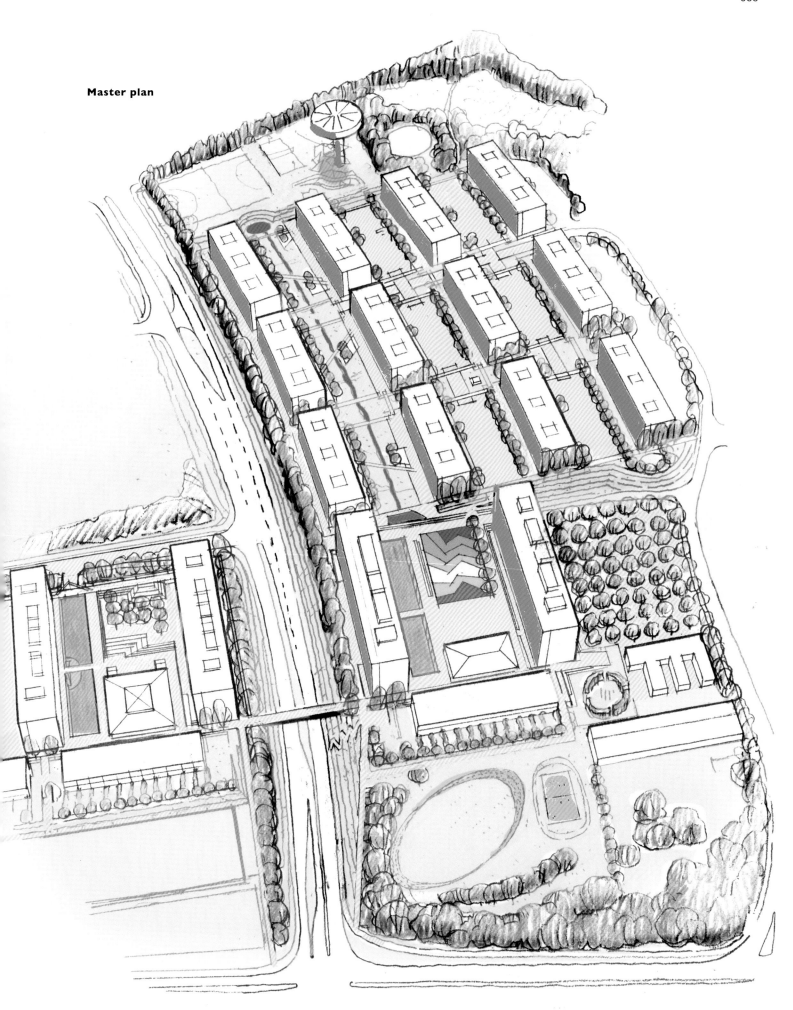

Site plan

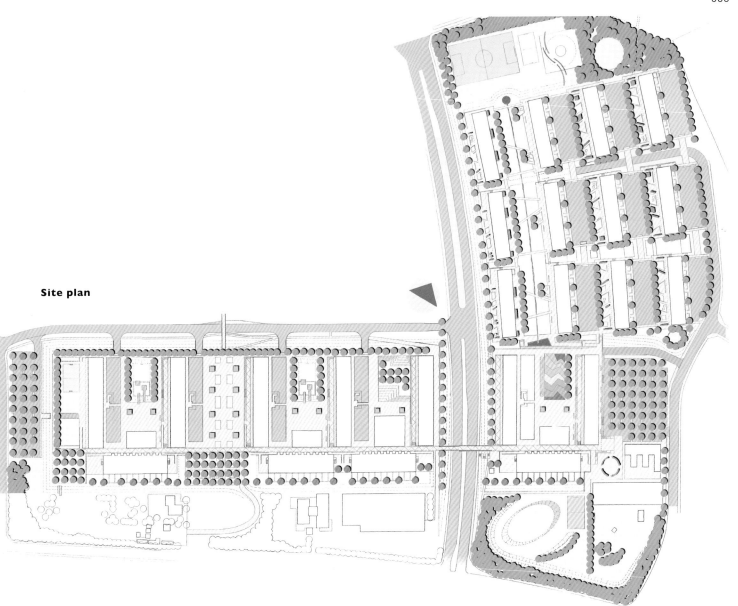

1. New meeting places for the residents
2-4. The open space is simple but comfortable

5. The new paving uses a restrained palette of black and white patterns
6-7. Details of the stairs
8-9. The plantings are equally kept simple with mainly wisteria, privet, various grasses and slender Himalayan birch trees

LODENAREAL

Location: Innsbruck, Austria
Design: Monsberger Gartenarchitektur
Photography: Monsberger Gartenarchitektur
Area: 24,500sqm

Combination of Urban and Landscape

The Stage – Window to the Landscape: The basic idea is to integrate the surrounding landscape as an identity feature. The increased grass platform takes on the role as mediator between the city (residential areas) and landscape (Inn) and leads the eye across to the mountains. Loosely strewn mountain ash is used as a landscape quote emphasises the character of this place.

Public Open Spaces

The Tape – Leisure and Recreation: The linear strip is zoned in the bank free from the natural environment in certain areas and certain urban and functional rooms. The immediate riparian zone is maintained as a gravel bank and open space and is flooded according to the water level temporarily. Stone body in the form of groynes provides direct access to the water at higher water levels. The dam is designed as an Inn promenade for pedestrians and cyclists. Chopped rear body structure in the south of the dam subsequent open space is formed as a function of volume (e.g. for beach volleyball, street ball, skating).

A single row of avenue planting (bird cherry) and the uniform planting of the embankment with sloes emphasises the linearity of the band and is interrupted only in the stage.

Free Space Residential Development

The Bar Code – Yellow, Red, Blue: Each courtyard is determined by a colour that gives it a distinctive character. Plants and materials in the basic colours yellow, red and blue colour determine the respective game. The change of seasons influenced the intensity of the colour in all its nuances.

The formal shape results from a free interplay of horizontal lines of the facade, like a bar code can be projected onto the surface area of the farms. Different areas give the code and allow a wide variety of uses.

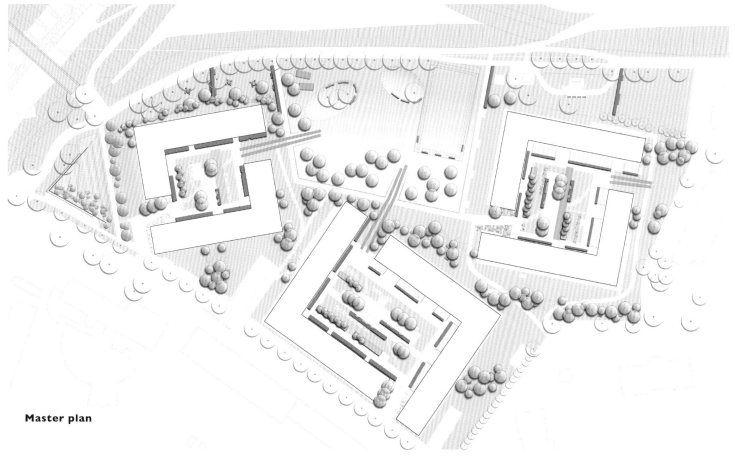

Master plan

2

1. Bird eye view
2. The increased grass platform takes on the role as mediator
3. Loosely strewn mountain ash is used as a landscape quote emphasizes the character of this place
4. The plants on the wooden deck

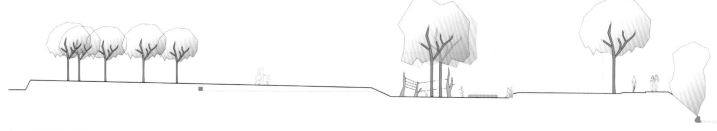

Concept drawing

5. Green lawn space for relaxing
6-7. The dam is designed as an Inn promenade for pedestrians and cyclists
8. The beach playground

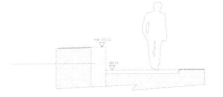

Sections

CSU FULLERTON HOUSING PHASE III

Location: Fullerton, CA, United States
Completion: 2011
Design: CMG: Landscape Architecture
Architect: Steinberg Architects
Photography: CMG: Landscape Architecture
Area: 36,423sqm

CMG collaborated with PCL Construction and Steinberg Architects for the design of this wining student housing competition entry. The extensive design/build proposal encompasses a long list of services in addition to student housing. Included in the proposal were student coordinator and faculty-in-residence apartments, administrative offices, conference and multi-purpose rooms, laundry and mail facilities, recreational lounges, a convenience store, a maintenance facility, a central plant, and a dining facility, along with 4 acres of new campus open space amenities on an 8.63 acre site. The landscape accommodates student activity of all scales, binds the new construction together as a district, and affords easy connections to the existing campus fabric.

The new heart of the campus housing district provides a large, flexible event space as well as a multitude of smaller gathering spaces for outdoor classrooms, study, and relaxation in the shade of broad canopy trees. All plant material is climate-appropriate, and stormwater quantity and quality control measures are fully integrated into the site design. The design team intends for the project to be LEED certified.

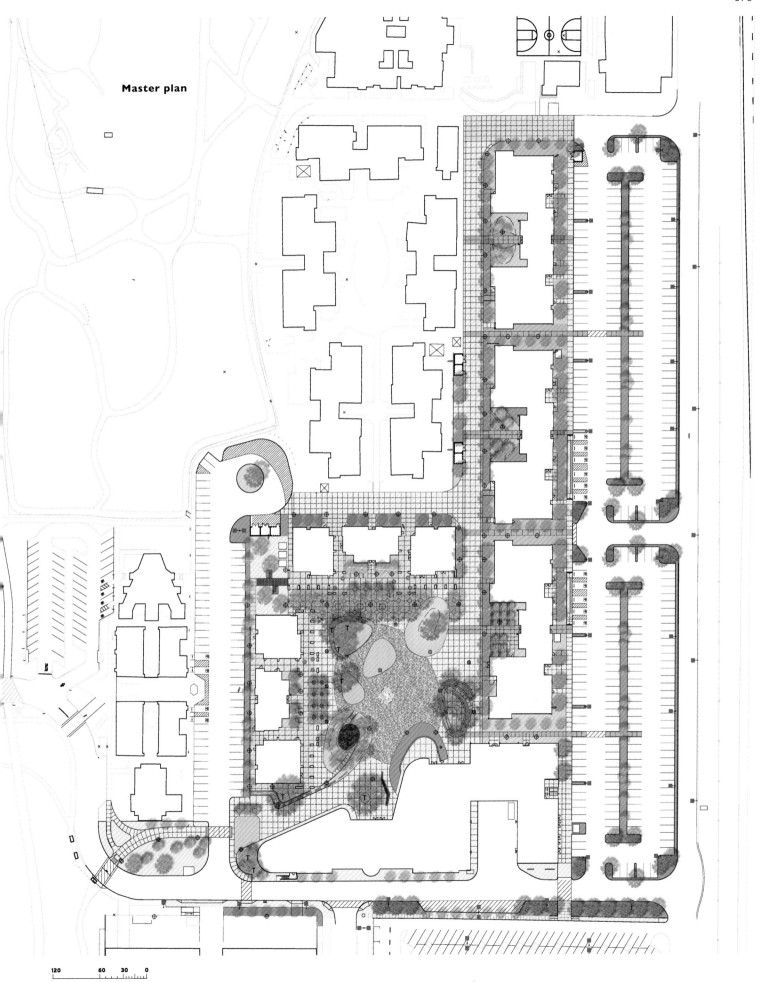

Master plan

1-2. The colourful pavement
3. Succulent plants
4. The fountain

5

5. The stone seatings
6-7. The wooden seatings
8. The plants chosen are climate appropriate

6

7

ROCKBROOK RESIDENTIAL COMPLEX

Location: Dublin, Ireland
Design: Bernard Seymour Landscape Architects
Photography: Derek Naughton
Area: 1,200sqm

This is a residential block, part of a much larger scheme, involving the master-planning and development of a district adjacent to Beacon South Quarter in Sandyford. The scheme is reasonably tall for the area, seven floors at its maximum, with two floors of underground car-parking. The challenge was to make a space of quality and utility for the residents where the sensation was of a courtyard in the most conventional sense, as opposed to some token greenery placed atop the car-park.

The concept was based on a woodland clearing, where one emerges from the shadows into a dappled area, where one can take advantage of the sunlight and warmth by resting a while on a fallen log. This fanciful notion had to be fused with the need to provide a useful amenity for the residents as the only communal space that they would all share.

A social space was desirable, with the conventional elements that might be expected, such as grass, seating, and a gathering area where residents might occasionally meet and put out some chairs and tables. Some greenery provided seasonality, scale and softness. The tricky part was not to make it look like planters placed above an underground car park, which is the reality of the project.

Master plan

1. Roadside, with designed ventilation grills
2. Overview
3. Bench with shadow gap

4. Path
5. Dynamic lines
6. Material detail
7. Cyclist
8. Variety of planting
9. Red Hot Pokers
10. Flowerbeds
11. Wheelchair ramp engulfed by vegetation

SUN CITY YOKOHAMA

Location: Yokohama, Japan
Design: SWA Group
Photography: Tom Fox
Area: 75,000sqm

Sun City Park Yokohama is a new CCRC (continuum of care retirement community) proposed for a site that had formerly been an explosives manufacturing facility in Hodogaya, a suburb of Yokohama, Japan. The project, to be operated by Health Care Japan Co., Ltd. (HCJ), a leader in Japan's fast growing senior housing and continuum care retirement communities, adds to an expanding portfolio of properties focused on housing Japan's growing senior population. This 7.5 hectare, former explosives manufacturing facility overlooking Yokohama provided a unique opportunity to allow the design team to formulate a master plan sensitive to the natural character and charm of this very unique site. The hilltop setting, woodland edges, and sensitive building layout, in conjunction with the introduced landscape present Sun City Yokohama as a landmark senior community in Japan.

With Perkins Eastman Architects PC, Pittsburgh, PA, SWA has completed the master planning phase of the project and is currently proceeding with schematic design. The plan consists of two single building "villages" connected by a pavilion-like community building. Each village has 240 Independent Living (IL) units, each with its own community living and dining programs. The west village also contains the 120-bed skilled nursing facility with its own arrival court on the north side of the building. The community building spans a natural draw in the landform that with the east village frames a large meadow that rolls toward a created stream that runs along the toe of a steep tree covered slope that forms the west edge of the space.

The residential wings of the villages extend into the landscape offering views into gardens, woodland preserve, and stunning distant views to Yokohama City to the east. The building composition thus frames a large stroll garden in the valley viewed from the main public rooms of both villages and residential units above, features a large open lawn and woodland understory garden separated by a gently cascading

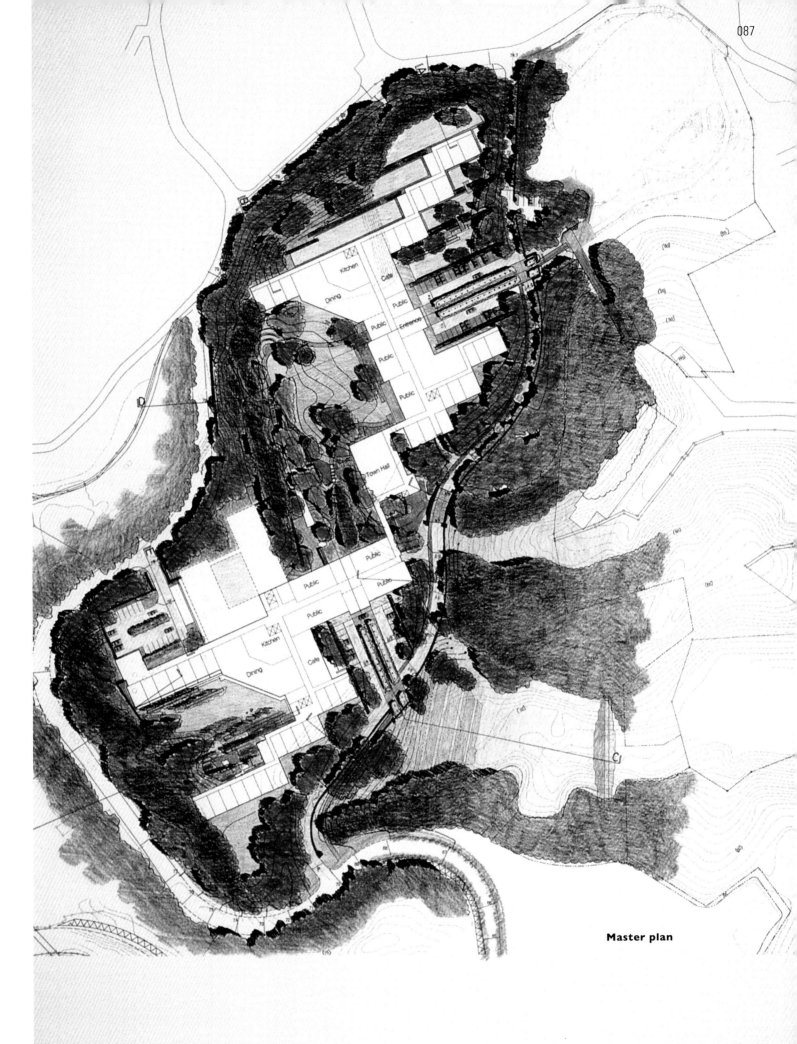

Master plan

1. Colourful flowers are planted
2. The community is like a garden
3. The path is wandering in the green plants

stream. For seniors, the compelling views of "garden" and nature from the buildings are an important part of everyday life, and perhaps as important as being in the landscape itself. The preserved and created landscapes of Sun City Park Yokohama meet that goal and more with a variety of outdoor spaces to accommodate various needs of the elderly including more active residents, as well as, larger group gatherings.

SWA's involvement in this project began with a feasibility study of the site and a review of the existing development scheme proposed by a competing senior housing developer.

The parcel size and context provides the opportunity to build a facility twice the size of any project in a truly park-like setting. The feasibility study confirmed that the previously proposed and approved unit count could be achieved without approaching the project as a terraced hillside development.

The greatest challenges for SWA are to sensitively grade the edges, to save existing mature trees and to design the project to maximise the use of existing site amenities. The entry road set below the pad elevation runs along the natural and partially wooded edge that will be reinforced to complete the "...through the woods to Grandmother's house we go" image.

4. The unique pavement
5. Concise and neat landscape
6. Seating place for relaxing
7. Green plants are good for relaxing

8. A created stream runs along the toe of a steep tree covered slope
9. A large meadow that rolls toward a created stream
10. Sensitive building layout is in conjunction with the introduced landscape
11. The ornamental landscape lighting

GREENCIA KAWASAKI-KYOMACHI

Location: Kawasaki, Japan
Completion: 2012
Design: Hiroshi Ishii (Yoshiki Toda Landscape
& Architect Co.,Ltd.)
Photography: Yoshiki Toda Landscape &
Architect Co.,Ltd.
Client: NIPPON STEEL KOWA REAL ESTATE
CO.,LTD., Nice Corporation, HASEKO
Corporation
Area: 14,587.48sqm

Landscape in a Grid

Located in Kawasaki-Kyomachi, Japan, GREENCIA Kawasaki-Kyomachi is an apartment development with 360 units. Now the block looks clean and neat, and the residential buildings combine with the park with natural landscape harmoniously, creating a calm and peaceful ambience. In a human-scale neighbourhood with over 100 years history, a lush apartment landscape of nearly 1.5 hectares which makes the best of the favourable conditions unfolds itself to the public.

Housing in Garden

It is noticeable that the project connects the enclosing spaces around the buildings and all the open spaces are open to public. If we say that residential buildings are everyday living places, outdoor spaces play an equal important role. The proposal aims to treat the surrounding outdoor space as a lush garden, through which man-to-man and man-to-nature direct contact happen. The ultimate goal is to create "Housing in Garden".

Six Landscape Gardens

The site is somewhat special because the distance from the front gate to the main entrance is about 180m. The architectural composition incorporates the irregular site and the main challenge of the preliminary phase is how to lead people to the main entrance area through landscape design. Generally speaking, the longer home-entry distance makes people feel alienated. However, with proper design, this disadvantage can create a charming path. In the programme, the landscape designers first apply some feature trees and rows of landscape trees at the end of

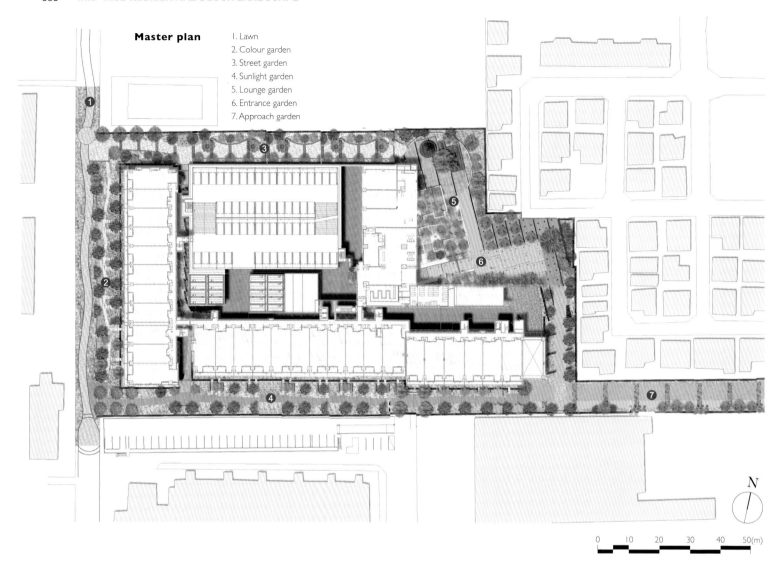

Master plan

1. Lawn
2. Colour garden
3. Street garden
4. Sunlight garden
5. Lounge garden
6. Entrance garden
7. Approach garden

N

0   10   20   30   40   50(m)

1. Entrance Garden – overlook of landscape axis at the entrance from main feature tree
2. Street Garden – landscape wall and small terrace in linear direction which provide space variation
3. Approach Garden – entrance columns and Cercidiphyllum border trees

the road leading to the front gate, which reduce people's resistance to distance through specific goals. Then, constant scene changes along the path create a pleasant pedestrian space. Meanwhile, seasonal plantings along the path enhance the landscape effect. In addition, the continuous outdoor space is divided into six areas. With different themes, the six gardens improve the circulation of the whole site and create continuous landscape in collocation with the terrain.

From Ornamental Garden to Living Garden

The gardens are not ornamental. Here, everyone can contact with nature and explore their own stories. The result is a living garden. The designers hope, in this delightful garden housing complex, human being, vegetation and other creatures will grow vigorously and here will become a valuable local landscape resource for the public to share.

4. Street Garden – waterside walkway which corresponds to curving landscape wall
5. Colour Garden – maple-based plantings and lawn create a soft image for the garden
6. Entrance Garden – shadows of border trees on the paving reflect the passage of time
7. Sunlight Garden – abundant sunlight and tree shade form a sunny grove

8. Lounge Garden – terraced garden which senses time from water pond, gravels and groundcover vegetation
9. Stone-faced feature wall of Approach Garden – main feature trees standing deep behind the rhythmic landscape walls
10. Entrance Garden – Cercidiphyllums and main feature trees at the main entrance
11. Entrance Garden – needle-leaved tress at the entrance

AVALON OCEAN AVENUE

Location: San Francisco, USA
Completion: 2012
Design: Jeffrey Miller (Miller Company
Landscape Architects)
Photography: Miller Company Landscape
Architects
Area: 30,263sqm

Avalon Ocean Avenue is a mixed-use residential and commercial development in the Balboa Park neighbourhood of San Francisco. This transit-oriented development is served by improved light rail and bus service along Ocean Avenue, as well as by the nearby Balboa Park BART station. The Ocean campus of the City College of San Francisco and the Ingleside branch of the San Francisco public library are immediately adjacent. Street-level retail includes a Whole Foods Market.

A pedestrian-oriented streetscape has been created along Ocean Avenue. Brighton Street extends into the development as an active "Woonerf" curbless street, with a raised terrace area that includes concrete seat walls and other pedestrian amenities. The street provides vehicles access to underground parking structures.

Residents can enter the building from the parking structure or through the street entry, which is flanked with palms in raised planters. Podium courtyards within the buildings create communal and private outdoor space for residents, with raised concrete planter boxes and a variety of fixed and movable seating.

The west podium features a wavy concrete bench and an outdoor cooking area with barbeques, a sink, and counters. Residents can enjoy a sunny day in the communal spaces, or sit in private patios on the ground level.

The east podium also allows for outdoor cooking and dining. It includes a dedicated space for gatherings with tables and chairs, as well as two comfortable seating areas around a fireplace. Raised planters provide some privacy and enliven the central space.

Site landscape plan

1. Residential lobby
2. Residential lobby
3. Ocean Avenue
4. Commercial lobby

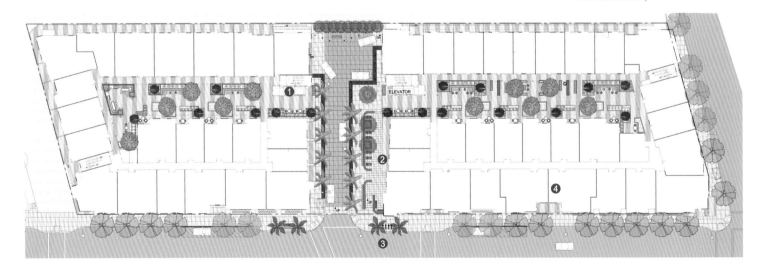

1. Patio east podium
2. Podium courtyards within the buildings
3. Raised concrete planter boxes
4. A variety of fixed and movable seating
5. A dedicated space for gatherings with tables and chairs

6

6. The west podium features a wavy concrete bench and an outdoor cooking area with barbeques
7-8. Residents can enter the building from the parking structure or through the street entry

VIA BOTANI

Location: Bangkok, Thailand
Completion: 2013
Design: Wannaporn Suwannatrai (Openbox Company Limited)
Photography: Wison Tungthunya
Area: 3,200sqm

VIA Botani is a medium size condominium at Sukhumvit Soi 47, which is considered to be right at the heart of Bangkok. The site is in a tranquil neighbourhood of private housing development from early time. One thing that contributes the most to the unique site character is a fully-grown, magnificent rain tree that stands tall in the middle of the land. This rain tree is where the whole story begins.

At first glance, design team agrees that the rain tree must be kept as a living feature to ensure success of the development. Since then, design process and development revolves intensely around the rain tree; starting from feasibility study, building layout all the way through construction process. Keeping a large size tree alive and well at the center of construction work is extremely difficult, but well worth it. In the end, the tree stands proudly as heroic-scaled, approaching feature that everyone will remember.

Another part of the landscape work is the 2nd courtyard that consists of swimming pool and pool deck area. Following the architectural façade concept, "Illusion", landscape features arise from illusive lines, forms, patterns, and grow into an intensive and colourful courtyard; fully functional, yet very pleasing to the eyes.

OPNBX's philosophy is about harmonising Architecture and Landscape. Although the architecture scope is by another design firm, close coordination unite the concept of building and surrounding into one, pursuing the same concept more powerfully. It is the concept that grows into value, the value of conserving one single tree, VIA Botani.

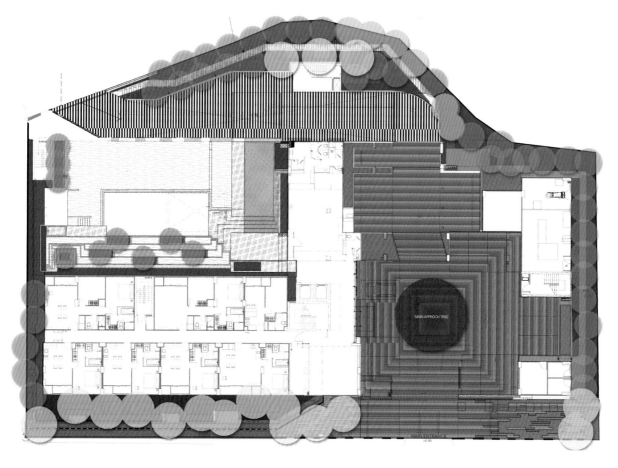

Landscape plan

1. The architectural façade concept arise from illusive lines, forms, patterns, and grow into an intensive and colourful courtyard
2. One thing that contributes the most to the unique site character is a fully-grown, magnificent rain tree
3. The featured green stairs
4. The tree pool
5. Paving detail

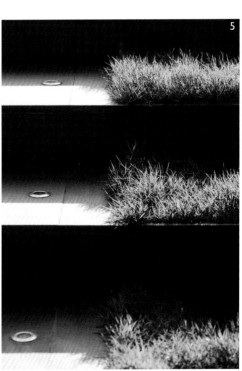

6

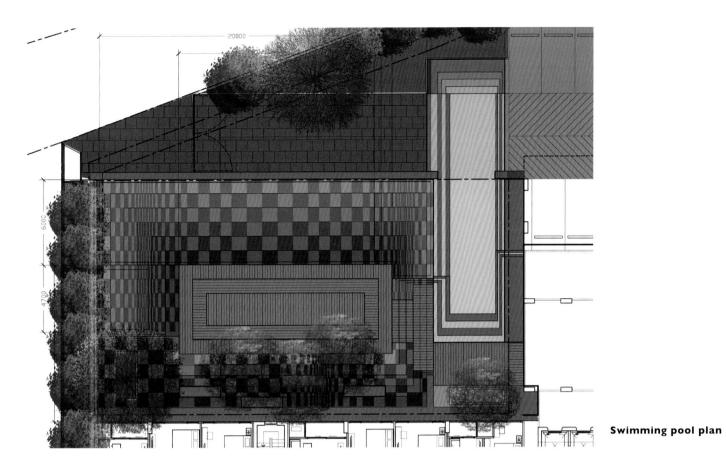

Swimming pool plan

6. The 2nd courtyard that consists of swimming pool and pool deck area
7-9. Details of the swimming pool and the deck

ASNIÈRES PUBLIC PARK

Location: Asnières sur Seine/France
Completion: 2012
Design: Espace Libre
Photography: Espace Libre
Area: 6,200sqm

Located in the heart of Asnières sur Seine, a plot of 6,000 m^2 on two levels becomes a meeting place for the population. As an urban staple it helps build a missing link between the different neighbourhoods, college and high school, which revolves around this space. To link the two sides of the square, a fold has achieved in the axis of the two entrances thereby making more natural path between them. Playgrounds surround the plot centre of the square, of which the top level, is reserved for children under 6 years, while the lower level is open to teens. A second square plot serves to college while acting as a gateway to the development. Moreover, a species-specific mono lavender, is planted on the edge of the high level to emphasise the link between the two entrances.

The designer strives to enhance the structural elements of the existing landscape, to make functional spaces while highlighting the social bond, to support the work done by opening up new networks and roads, to showcase strong areas and centralists, as well as developing the attractiveness of equipped sites.

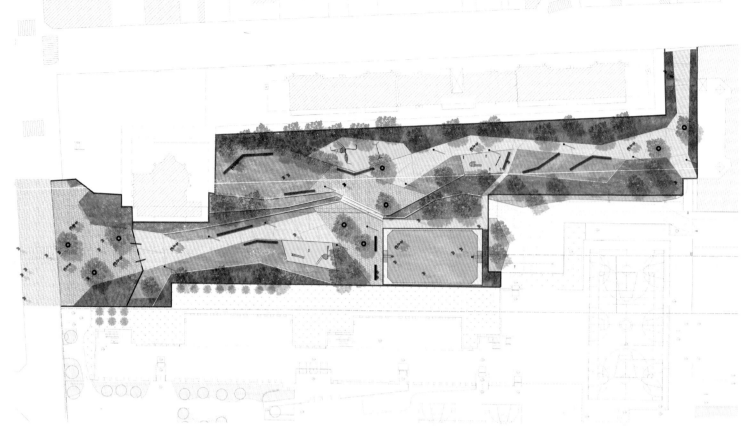

Plan drawing

Impression drawing

1. Overview of the public park
2-3. Playgrounds surround the plot centre of the square
4-5. Paving details

ATHLETESVILLAGE PLOT N13 & N26 LANDSCAPE – PODIUM GARDENS

Location: London, UK
Completion: 2012
Design: C.F. Møller Architects
Client: ODA (Olympic Delivery Agency), LendLease
Area: 7,000sqm (podium gardens)

The key objective for the podium garden landscapes of the plots N13 and N26 of the Athletes Village has been to re-create lost ecology values, in a once ecologically rich region. This is in accordance with the Stratford City Masterplan and the Site Wide Biodiversity objectives for the Olympic village. The landscape design seeks to create an urban woodland, in the broadest sense of the word, with geographical and historical references to the borough of Waltham Forest and the adjacent southernmost fringes of Epping Forest.

Hence the landscape design sets the plots in the wider landscape context of the Lea Valley, Epping Forest and the open spaces of London as whole. Within the scheme the designers have achieved a rich diversity of habitats to attract wildlife to the urban setting.

The planting strategy uses a largely native palette of species encouraging biodiversity and providing a human scale to the courtyards. In order to enable planting of semi-mature woodland species, with possibility for future growth on the podium deck the design concept is based on forming a series of green hillocks. These have the dual purpose of accommodating the resident's needs for outdoor recreation in a diverse landscape and at the same time maximising the growth potential for the maturing trees. Imbedded within the lawns are ornamental and space defining beds with tall grasses and lavender planting, interconnected with tree groves and hills.

A path paved with yellow bricks threads through the courtyard creating a visual and functional connection between the built architecture and the landscape spaces. The hillocks references to the wider landscape context and simultaneously they provide identifiable orientation features to the courtyards.

The position of the individual woodland hills' is situated in accordance to provide shelter for the exposed eastern elevation of the courtyard whilst the large trees reinforce a sense of unity between the two plots architectural forms. The juxtaposition of consistency and contrast between landscape and built architecture creates a rich, subtle and engaging environment.

1. The landscape design seeks to create an urban woodland
2. Bird eye view

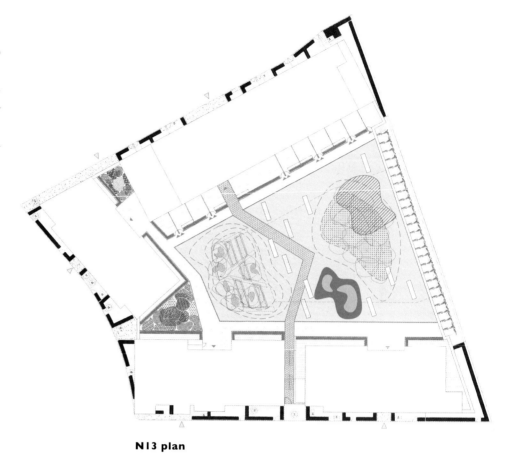

N13 plan

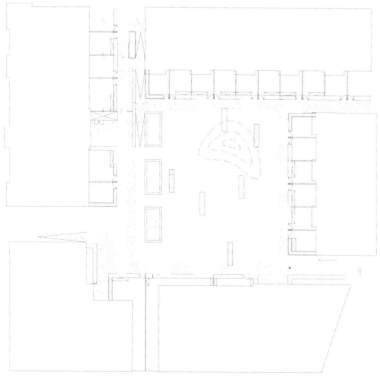

N26 plan

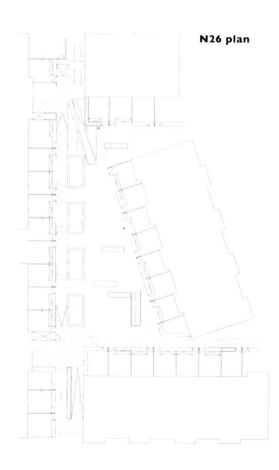

N26 plan

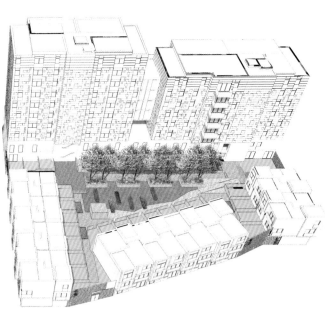

3. A series of green hillocks
4-5. A diverse landscape for outdoor recreation
6. Embedded within the lawns are ornamental and space defining beds with tall grasses and lavender planting
7. A path paved with yellow bricks threads through the courtyard

•High-rise residential tower landscape

THE INTERLACE

Location: Singapore
Completion: 2013
Landscape Designer: OMA (Concept/SD) /
ICN Design International Pte Ltd., Singapore
Design Architect: OMA / Ole Scheeren
Photography: Iwan Baan
Area: 170,000sqm

The 170,000 m² development, which was completed and handed over to residents in late 2013, provides 1,040 generous residential units of varying sizes that are reasonably priced. The unusual geometry of the hexagonally stacked building blocks creates a dramatic spatial structure populated by a diverse array of activity areas.

Eight expansive courtyards and their individual landscapes are defined as the heart of the project and form distinct spatial identities. Each courtyard, spanning a distance of 60m across and extending further through the permeable interconnections, possesses a specific character and atmosphere that serves as a place-maker and spatial identifier.

The primary pedestrian route through the project leads residents from the main entrance through and to the courtyards as primary points of orientation and identification – you live in a courtyard, a space, rather than a building or an object. Pedestrian circulation is grouped and bundled according to the density of residents around each courtyard in a central "connector". A system of secondary footpaths brings residents from the connector to the private front doors of their homes.

The Interlace generates a space of collective experience within the city and reunites the desire for individual privacy with a sense of togetherness and living in a community. Social interaction is integrated with the natural environment in a synthesis of tropical nature and habitable urban space.

The notion of community life within a contemporary village is emphasised throughout the project by an extensive network of communal gardens and spaces. A variety of public amenities are interwoven into the landscape, offering numerous opportunities for social interaction and shared activities integrated with the natural environment.

A Central Square, Theatre Plaza, and Water Park occupy the more public and

1. Bird eye view
2. The unnsual geometry of the hexagonally stacked buildings creates a dramatic spatial structure

central courtyards and contain numerous shared amenity areas such as a clubhouse, function and games rooms; theatre, karaoke, gyms, and reading rooms; and a 50m lap pool and sun deck, family and children's pools. Surrounding courtyards such as The Hills and Bamboo Garden provide shaded outdoor play and picnic areas with lower blocks around its perimeter. The Waterfall, Lotus Pond, and Rainforest Spa complete the eight main courtyards and offer residents further choices and areas in a more contemplative environment with additional swimming pools, spa gardens, and outdoor dining.

Multiple barbeque areas, tennis and multicourts, organic garden, pet zone, and "the rock" line the perimeter of the project and offer a wide selection of communal activities for residents. A continuous loop around the site provides a 1km running track and connects the "internal" courtyards to the activities around the edge of the site.

The character of a vertical village embedded in a rich landscape of activities and nature is evident throughout the project. Elevated roof terraces and sky gardens extend outdoor space on multiple levels with views above the tree line to the surrounding courtyards, parks, sea, and city. The diversity of the various offerings and atmospheres of natural environment encourage social interaction with the freedom of choice for different gradients of privacy and sharing, contributing to the overall sense of community.

Sustainability features are incorporated throughout the project through careful

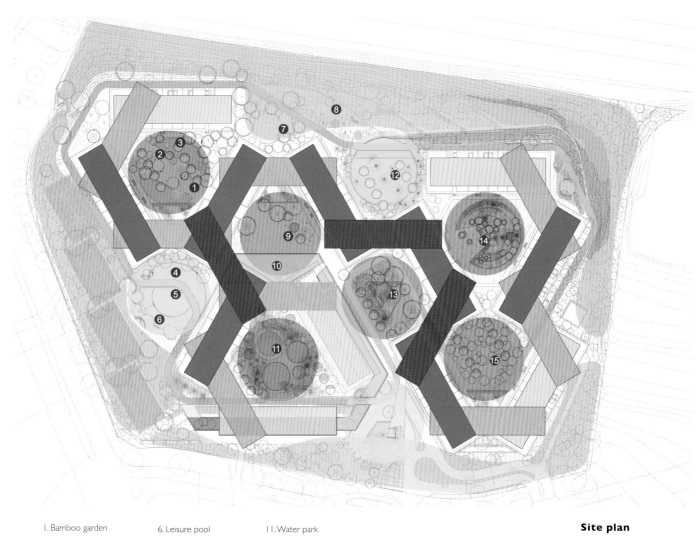

Site plan

1. Bamboo garden
2. Stone garden
3. Seating areas
4. Reflection pond
5. Water fall
6. Leisure pool
7. Organic garden
8. Play zone
9. Theatre plaza
10. Gymnasium
11. Water park
12. Lotus pond
13. Central square
14. Rainforest
15. The hills

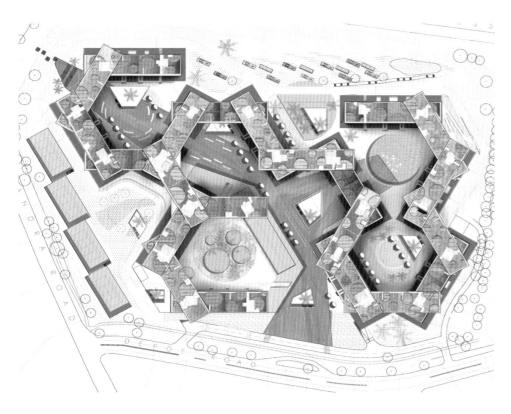

The roof scape

3. Dramatic spatial structure populated by a diverse array of activity areas
4. The swimming pool
5. Pedestrian circulation is grouped and bundled
6. A variety of public amenities are interwoven into the landscape
7. Night view of the community

environmental analysis and integration of low-impact passive energy strategies. A series of site specific environmental studies, including wind, solar, and daylight analysis, were carried out to determine intelligent strategies for the building envelope and landscape design. As a result, the project has been awarded the Universal Design Mark Platinum Award and Green Mark Gold Award from Singapore's Building and Construction Authority.

MIRO

Location: Singapore
Completion: 2013
Design: ONG&ONG Pte Ltd
Photography: See Chee Keong
Area: 14,191sqm

Miro is a high-rise residential development located within close proximity to Singapore's bustling areas of Orchard Road and Little India. It maximises the site's limited land area through an effective use of space and uses lush landscaping to give its urban buildings a touch of nature.

By placing the approach to the site via the relatively quiet Keng Lee Road, the drive up to Miro feels akin to being on a private driveway with a tree-lined boulevard. The road is further accentuated by linear latticed trellises teeming with luxuriant green creepers and giving the boundary wall a more porous and natural feel. These trellises run all the way up to the entrance podium and culminate in a grand reception structure, while an inclined water feature on the ground level welcomes visitors.

.Plants on the trellis' green wall are supported by an in-built irrigation system, which also helps to clear dissolved pollutants in the water. In addition, the trellis' green wall not only enhances the façade's aesthetic appeal but also brings down the building's temperature and keeps its surroundings cool.

The first and second storeys are set aside for group interaction and activities, with the latter serving as a spa haven and an extension of one's living space. This idea of an extended living space can also be seen in the landscaped terraces on the 3rd, 9th, 13th, 17th, 21st, 25th and 29th storeys. Each sky terrace has an integrated pantry for residents to dine in the garden pavilions, which are filled with a variety of plants that support a community of butterflies and birds.

The melding of city life with natural, green elements makes Miro a resort-like haven in the heart of Singapore.

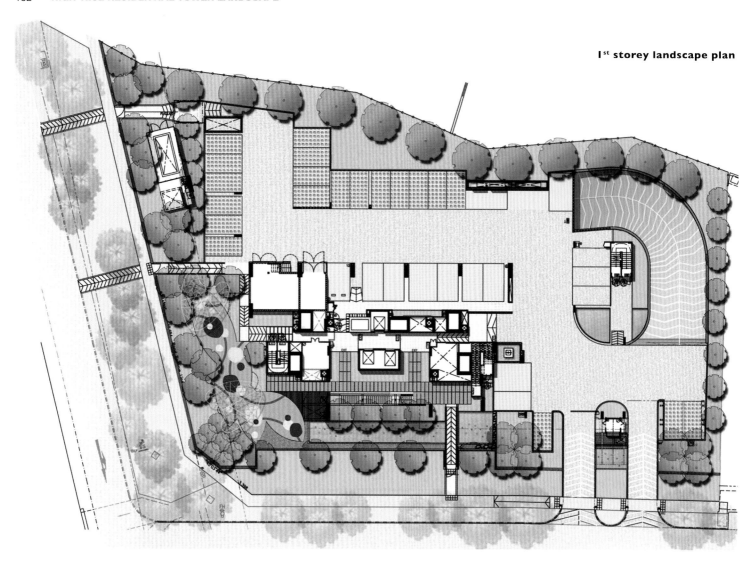

1st storey landscape plan

1. The drive up to Miro feels akin to being on a private driveway with a tree-lined boulevard
2. The road is accentuated by linear latticed trellises teeming with luxuriant green creepers
3. Water feature
4. Retaining wall
5. Garden bed

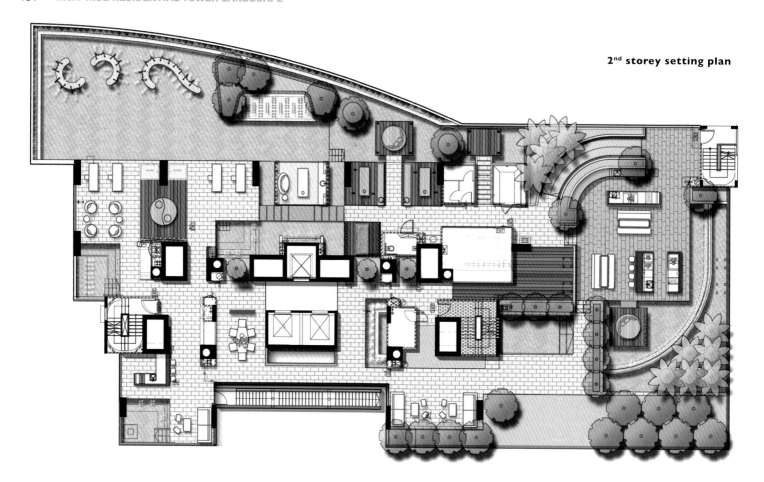

2nd storey setting plan

6. Garden pavilions
7. A variety of plants that support a community of butterflies and birds
8-9. An inclined water feature on the ground level welcomes visitors

SOLEIL@SINARAN

Location: Singapore
Completion: 2011
Design: Tierra Design (S) Pte Ltd
Photography: Amir Sultan
Area: 12,469sqm
Award: FIABCI Prix d'Excellence International Award 2013 – Silver Winner in the Residential High Rise Category

Going Urban to Suburban in Five Minutes

The Soleil condominium project lies right in the middle of one of the busiest parts of Singapore, and consequently, presented challenges from this perspective. How do you take a tenant or visitor from urban jungle to suburbia just by turning off a street?

To do this, the designers first moved the residential buildings as far as possible from the busiest road, and then lowered the car park into the basement to provide more space for design features at the entry level. This area was then covered in tropical plants and water features.

Visitors walking into the space from the busy street are immediately greeted with covered walkways that meander through the large pools and surrounding greenery, quickly putting them at ease and separating them from the hustle and bustle outside. They can walk in utter privacy and peace to their homes without prying eyes from the residents already comfortably situated above.

From the top, residents are treated to a "fifth elevation", that ensures a large undisturbed view of green and blue. The gazebo roofs are covered in curvilinear patterns of varied planting that allow observers an interesting change with the seasons. To provide variety, some plants sprout to life in the summer and others in the monsoon, making the view different at different times of the year.

The swimming areas for adults and children are separated, with smaller, shallower play areas reserved for children that are closer to the sheltered walkways and barbeque areas. Here parents can safely bask in the shelter while also looking over their children as they play.

Master plan

1. Entry landscape for car park
2-3. Covered walkways that meander
through the large pools and surrounding
greenery

4. Residents can enjoy a large undisturbed
view of green and blue from the top
5. The swimming pool
6. The shelter besides the swimming pool
7-8. Lush green plants and quiet paths

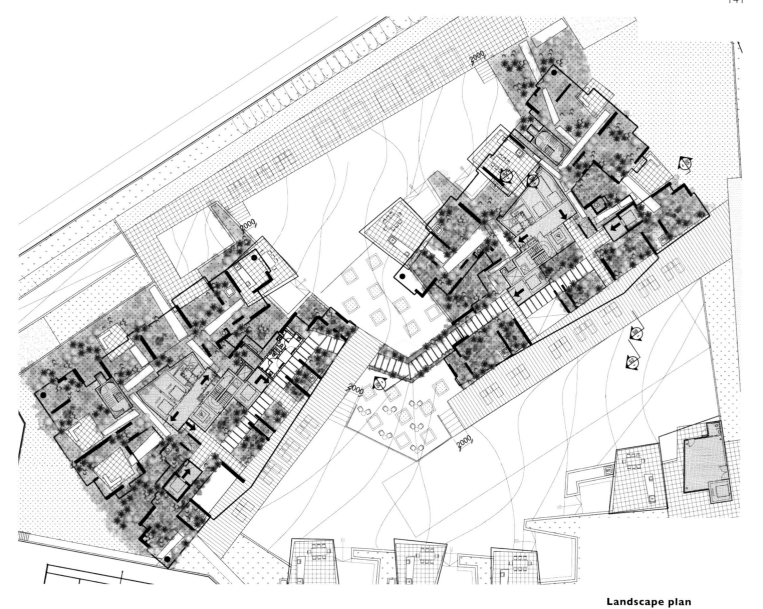

Landscape plan

8 NAPIER ROAD

Location: Singapore
Completion: 2012
Design: Tierra Design
Photography: Amir Sultan
Area: 6,774sqm

The landscape design of 8 Napier was built around accommodating and minimising the steep incline of the property. Flanked by a seven metre high wall on one side and the wall of a hospital building on the other, the design focuses on minimising views of the concrete and maximising emphasis on the greenery while moving through the property.

The generous forecourt at the entrance of the property is further enhanced by the placement of three aged Syzigium trees. These trees anchor the forecourt, creating an effortless and beautiful transition from the busy street into the property. Against a monochromatic backdrop, the rugged stone feature contrasts against the orthogonal surfaces of the pond and the property.

8 Napier is located in a very impressive part of town. Standing at 10 storeys high, comprising a total of 46 units, the architecture strives for serene simplicity as expressed by its clean, modernist lines. The indistinguishable boundary of indoor and outdoor living is elegantly composed and conceived as one. Landscape design for the scheme had to be there presentation of the unique character of the site and is in close proximity to the existing site setting, i.e. the level difference from front to rear of the site and the natural scenic qualities that the site enjoys. The design is an attempt to create a series of spatial experiences to mediate the seven metres from the entry plaza to the highest pool deck level.

The design concept derives naturally from the physical nature of the site, sloping up from south to north from Napier Road to Nassim Hill. In a series of large, gently rising terraces, beginning from the entrance courtyard porte-cochere, Napier Residences orchestrates its experiences one wonderful landscaped level at a time. Tranquil reflecting ponds and gently overflowing waters create soothing sounds, culminating at a luxurious swimming pool. The entrance courtyard is a generous space anchored by an inviting canopy which seems to levitate over a verdant green "wall" bathed in natural light. This green planting wall, together with the reflecting, overflowing pond, forms the main focus of the porte-cochere. Three large Syzygium

2

gratum trees anchor the plaza with the pond. Ten Plumeria trees with other surrounding lush green foliage, enhance the welcoming entrance plaza court experience.

1. The landscape design was built around accommodating and minimising the steep incline of the property
2. The high wall climbing with lush plants
3. The indistinguishable boundary of indoor and outdoor living is elegantly composed and conceived as one
4. The vertical green wall

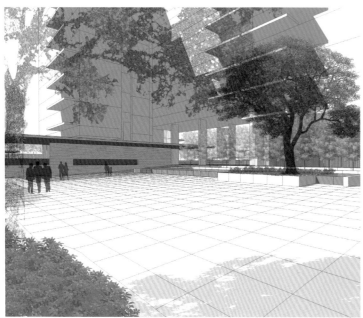

3

4

5

6

7

147

5. The reflection pool
6. The shelter besides the pool
7. The swimming pool
8. Night view of the stairs

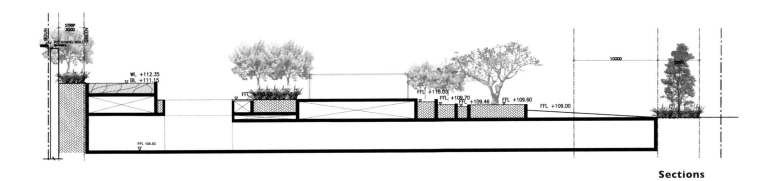

Sections

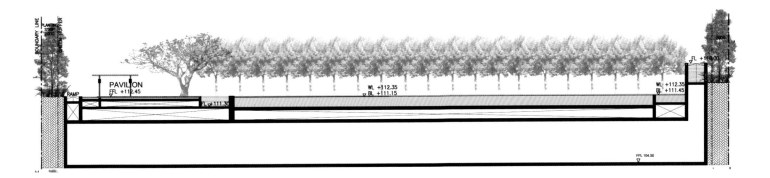

WATERFRONT KEY

Location: Singapore
Completion: 2012
Design: ONG&ONG Pte Ltd
Photography: See Chee Keong
Area: 19,980sqm

Located next to Singapore's Bedok Reservoir, Waterfront Key comprises of 8 blocks of 15-storey residential blocks and the site enjoys a beautiful panoramic view of the reservoir. The concept for its landscape design was to incorporate the nearby reservoir into the condominium's setting, thus making it seem like an extension from the site. Outward-facing units along Bedok Resorvoir Road will have the reservoir views while inward-looking units will be able to enjoy the central water court.

Forming the central spine of the linear water court are the lagoon and lap pools. A section of the pool deck is designed to look like a beach with a line of coconut trees leading up to where the sand gradually meets the water. This design allows to walk comfortably into the shallow water – a feature that takes into consideration the safety needs of the young, elderly and those are less confident of swimming.

Flanking this beach entry are two lushly landscaped islands with specially designed pavilion suites. These suites are available for private parties, whereby the entire island can be leased out. Each pavilion suite comprises a lounge and dining salon with a fully-fitted open kitchen. Here, one may have a soiree with friends under the stars whilst lounging by the pool with a glass of wine.

The lagoon and lap pools occupy almost three-quarters of the water court's length, culminating in the family-oriented zone where children's splash pool, aqua gym and hydrotherapy pool are clustered.

Adjacent to these pools is the clubhouse – a two-storey, linear structure that houses the gym, multi-purpose function room, steam bath as well as shower rooms. In front of the clubhouse are two tennis courts, while the clubhouse's roof terrace houses more cooking and dining facilities. A jogging circuit was also paved along the green areas of the site's periphery, and this allows avid joggers to warm up sufficiently before a run around the reservoir.

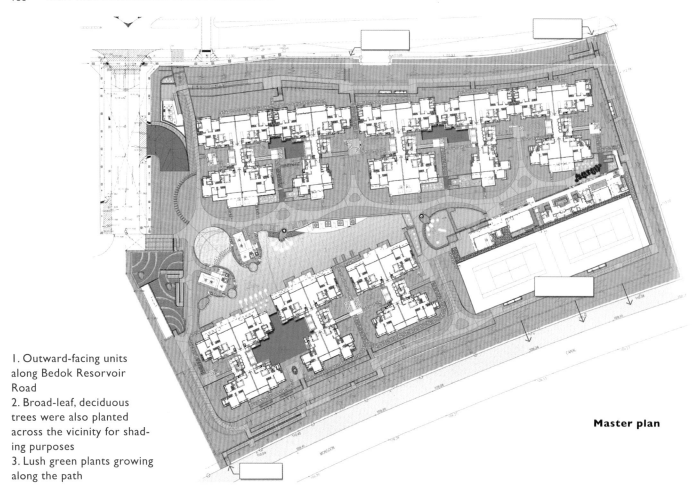

Master plan

1. Outward-facing units along Bedok Resorvoir Road
2. Broad-leaf, deciduous trees were also planted across the vicinity for shading purposes
3. Lush green plants growing along the path

4

4. A conducive environment for residents
5. The harmonious and seamless interphase between the verdant landscape

Interesting spatial experiences have been created through the harmonious and seamless interphase between the verdant landscape, hardscape and buildings. They have been designed to provide a conducive environment as well as opportunities for chance encounters to forge friendship in addition to family bonding.

Natural elements have been incorporated within the premises for both pragmatic and aesthetic purposes. For instance, creepers, instead of synthetic materials, were used as natural sun-shading screens for the walkways. Broad-leaf, deciduous trees were also planted across the vicinity

5

6. The open plaza
7-8. Playground
9. Pavilion suites
10. The featured pavement on the pool
11. The pool deck
12. Lushly landscaped islands
13. The water feature in the pool

for shading purposes. Other green measures adopted were the use of energy-efficient LED lights in water features and walls.

Waterfront Key, with its lush landscape, captures the essence of a sleepy fishing village found in the early days, while modern-day comforts necessary for contemporary living are well provided within the premise.

39 BY SANSIRI CONDOMINIUM

Location: Bangkok, Thailand
Design: Shma Company Limited
Photography: Wison Tungthanya
Area: 2,400sqm

39 by Sansiri is a high-end condominium development in one of the busiest districts of Bangkok. Being in such prime location, building footprint occupies most of the site to maximise residential area. Outdoor space becomes an integral part of the building itself with parts of the space being covered by roof. The concept is to define this intermediate space between exterior and interior.

In order to construct a tall building in limited area, architecture is built up on wide but thin columns to maximise functioning space. Likewise, landscape is designed to perform well with architectural language, by an extrusion of outdoor space that carves into a lobby interior visually connected through transparent glass wall. And the pool on level 9, elongates above landscape and surpasses beyond building façade, which seems to be floating in the sky.

As well as an interior language was adapted into landscape design, trimmed bush and ground covers were arranged in dynamic dimension to form spatial space; concrete structures become walls and seats, creating isolate sanctuary that is set apart by green lawn and water platforms. A threshold from open yard to lobby is a long corridor with water feature on both side, accommodating an ambience effect which soothes residents who pass by. Continuous glass wall of the lobby that pushed further in is not only replenishing the lack of outdoor area but also visually connecting an experience when moving through.

On level 9, a pool extends toward the east where it is an entrance to building. An actual pool structure is cantilevered to provide lap length and extension to city

Master plan

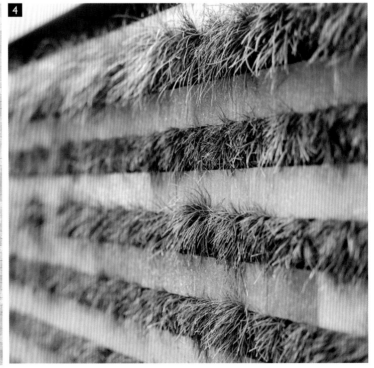

views. Water body stands in the middle between sun beds on wood deck and private pavilions which place isolated on water. By facing east, architecture benefits landscape through having proper sunlight flooded the entire floor. In addition, with open wall design, the area will always receive cool breeze from the south which is essential to Thailand. Wind flows across the pavilions onto water, its surface conceives vibration then remedial treatment occurs.

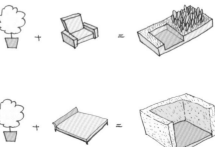

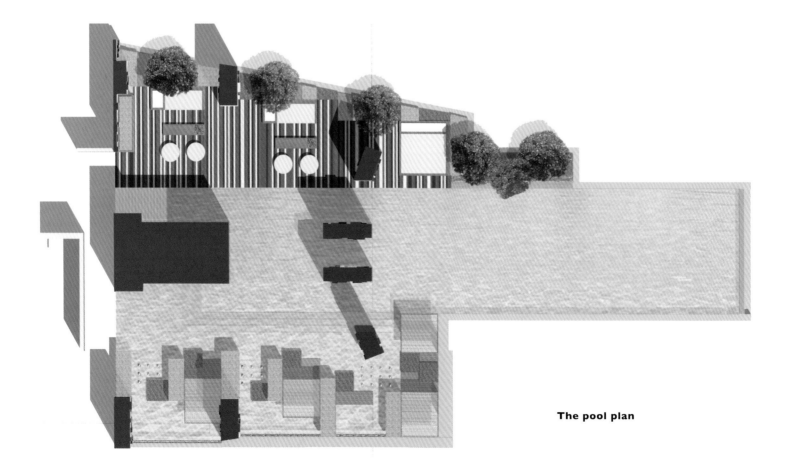

The pool plan

8

For sculpturous feature, the water pavilions are finished by porous pattern woods and green hedge around it to form a personal island. Each of it stands alone on water surface that sunken at angle depth. Resting is more dramatic when each pavilion contains a private Jacuzzi that connects from adjacent pool, accessible from water deck or pavilion seats.

At night when all the lights up, central stair core that sits at the pool edge has turned into a tall lantern. Warm light suffuse through its translucent wall and the pool reflect glares along with scattered dot lights installed at pool floor. Therefore, this cantilever pool

becomes a star ocean soothing all residents above them.

Furthermore, landscape details are also reflected upon finished materials and pavements. All tiles align accordingly to a direction where circulation will flow smoothly in a space. Paving on partition is vertically aligned while abstractions of natural stone that appear in dynamic depth and width of each tile also convey organic matter into architecture. A continuum materials decision from inside to outside based on a compromising between interior and landscape designers, to enhances the space's fluidity.

7. The pool on level 9 seems to be floating in the sky
8. Water body stands in the middle between sun beds on wood deck and private pavilions

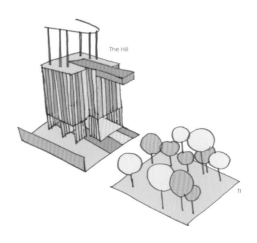

THE BASE

Location: Bangkok, Thailand
Completion: 2013
Design: Shma Company Limited
Photography: Wison Tungthunya, Santana Petchsuk
Area: ground floor green area: 2,363.7sqm
4th floor green area: 743.8sqm

People's lifestyle tends to have higher demand for individual space, while living in the densely populated district where space is limited. Condominium is one of the new. Vertical living is always the most effective solution in all cases. The extra facilities platforms are strategically added to extend the recreational space, to interlock various function together, and to form small gatherings within community. Recreational and sport facilities space are welded to each other by stripe paving patterns while selected planting palette binds landscape space as a whole. Green is also vertically linked to encourage people to use the space more productively.

As this high rise situated aligned a small street on one side and a canal bridge on the other, landscape embraces these residential units all around. Landscape specifically raised into multiple levels to serves at various functions. Therefore, the lowest ground continues from entrance toward all routes for 3 different platforms.

First route leads to an outdoor terrace, where it is extended out of the building cover, becaming a waiting platform for laundry service where parents can watch kids play on the lower ground. The second route keeps the same lowest ground height to all pockets of recreational platforms, from basketball court, kid's playground, to a more private gathering at another side of the building. The third route rises at seat height for the lowest ground, the platform is filled with green lawns and sand wash finished as some edge become seating. This last route runs along the outer edge of overall landscape that leads people to the last platform of a health exercise path with mini soccer field. All routes are completed as a full loop.

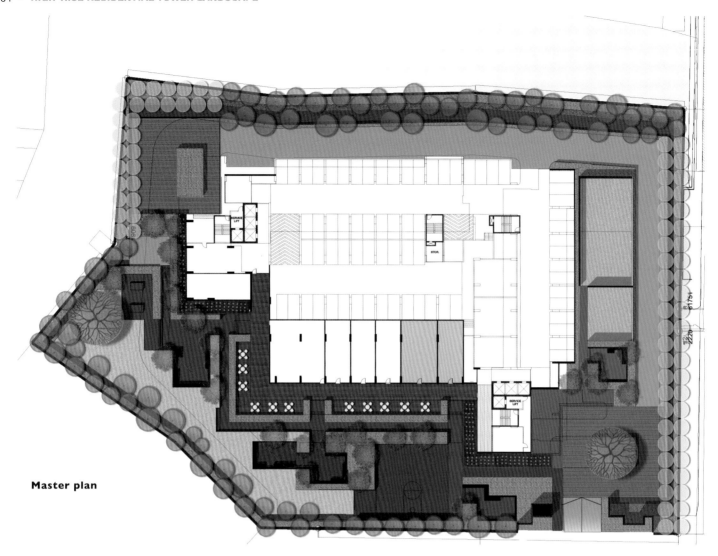

Master plan

1. Bird eye view of the swimming pool
2. The playground

Walking around these loops makes sense when relax environment occurs. From an intense daily routine of city people, landscape not only alleviates mental health but also turns into a hangout place for friends and family. Green tall bush covers the entire concrete wall that is used for privacy. The tall bamboos alongside the vertical bridge are spanned a flowing curtain, which also provide serene sound ambience to its surroundings. Within the project's landscape is a continuous flow for an overall visual connectivity at the maximum scale.

Consequently, the same strategy was applied to the pool and other recreational services on 4th floor. Matrix unit slightly distributes between resting and swimming area yet bonding the two different functions in an enjoyable experience.

Landscape on 4th floor also is divided into 3 platforms: an Active Platform, to hide away active moments of fitness, walkway and lounge behind the semi enclosure of vertical wood fins. Pool Platform with seating cuddling in trees and bushes, placed where can be perceived from all resident levels. Flexible green platform, with only transparent glass walls that block the pool deck and cityscape.

Ultimately, the strategy of extra facility platform is used to achieve the goal. Landscape elements also are expressed in various tones of blue to create the atmosphere of youth, dynamic, energy, and mysteriousness which are out interpretation for the metropolitan character. The project not only creates a living space, it forms the community.

3. Landscape embraces these residential units all around
4. The green plants along the path
5. Green tall bush covers the entire concrete wall that is used for privacy
6. Sand wash finished as some edge become seating
7. The platform is filled with green lawns

8. The water feature
9. The swimming pool
10. Green platform

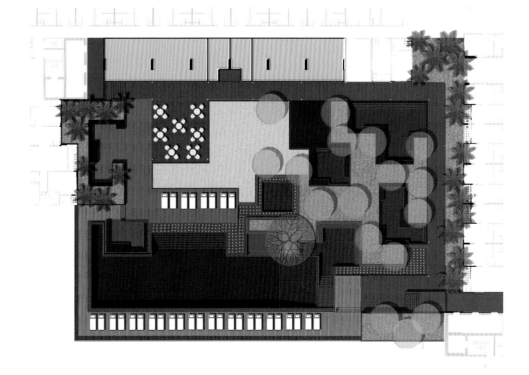

Pool plan

BLOCS 77 CONDOMINIUM

Location: Bangkok, Thailand
Design: Shma Company Limited
Photography: Mr. Wison Tungthanya
Area: 5, 244sqm

Blocs 77: Green Camouflage

Blocs 77 is an affordable condominium project located closely to the sky-train at one of the busiest urban area in Bangkok. The project plot is 5,244sqm and comprises of 467 residential units. The project is surrounded by many shop houses, shopping mall, and serene canal. In the front of the site, the project is facing a busy street with the traffic congestion all day; while at the back of the site, it is facing a peaceful canal and an old residential compound located on the opposite side of the canal. The rising trend of real-estate development along the sky-train route has transformed the existing low-rise houses and shop houses to the high-rise condominiums. There is the regulation of providing 6 metres fire engine route around the building and the requirement of on ground parking lots. All of which must be in a hard surface. In order to comply with the regulation and requirement, the mass of new condominium not only dominates its overall tight site and neighbours but also increases heat and glare reflecting from the building and hard surfaces around the building to the surrounding context.

Other constraints that this project is facing are the flooding during the rainy season, the high groundwater level within the site, and the limited space on the facility floor. To deal with these constraints, the landscape design approach is focused on making this project green as much as possible in order to minimise the impact of the heat and glare from the hard surfaces, raising the planting area above the existing grade level to avoid the root ball to contact with the groundwater directly, and providing sunken space to control the flooding. The designers use the concept of "tree canopy" as a metaphor of nature which helps camouflage the development with green spaces horizontally and vertically.

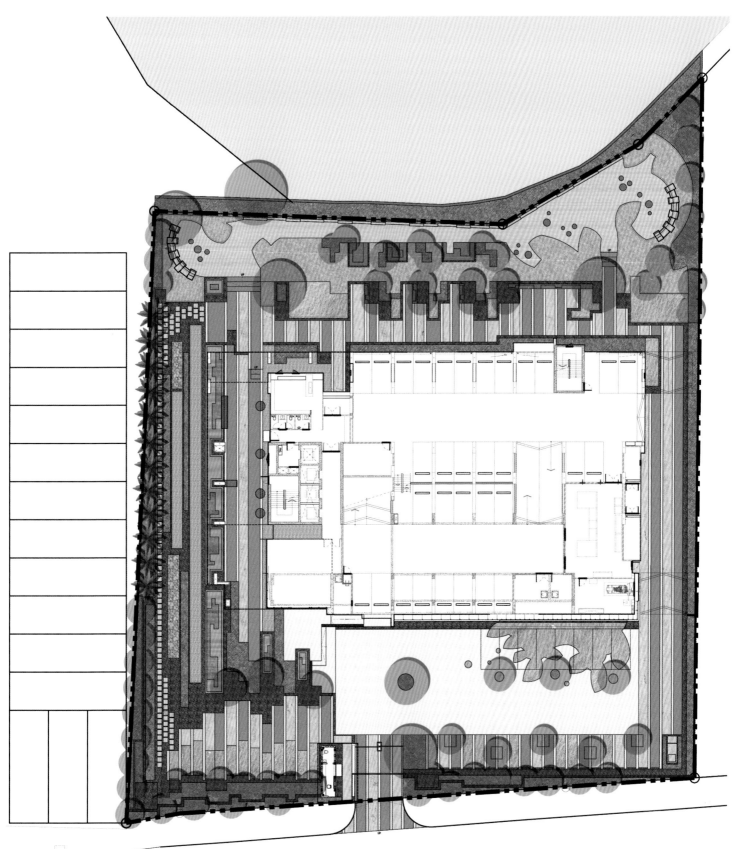

Master plan

Design Approach

1. Turning Hard into Green

In this project, fire engine route, parking lots, and plaza areas are covered in permeable surface of turf pave and gravel. These materials help soften the environment visually, reduce water run-off, and make these areas become more pleasant and welcome. The silhouette form of the tree canopy is used in turf pave area at the arrival court which becomes a signature of the project. At the vertical plane of the building, the

landscape designers work closely with architect in order to locate the series of planters at the parking podium as well as at the residential tower. The overhanging planters at the building façade offer opportunity for the residents to get closer to nature while the planters at the parking podium help absorb carbon dioxide (CO_2) from cars. These vertical green elements not only create the unique character of the building but also reduce heat and glare from the building to its surrounding, and therefore, lead to a good environment

of the city.

2. Raising above the Water Level

As the site location is adjacent to the canal and the change in urban planning from the previous permeable surface to the hard surface environment, these factors have an impact to the high groundwater level within the site which results in the difficulty in draining stormwater into the ground, the increase of water run-off, and the survival of many plant species. To solve the problem, the designers raise most

of the planter areas above the ground by 450 mm to avoid root ball to contact with the groundwater directly or submerge in the water during the heavy rainfall. These elevated planters are not used as the groundwater protection but are functioned as the sculptural seating, forming outdoor room for recreational purposes.

3. Edge Condition
This project is facing public areas on two sides. One is the busy road at the front and another is the tranquil canal at the back. The design approach is to maintain the continuity of the green area along both sides as much as possible. At the front edge adjacent to the street, the designers propose to set the boundary wall about 2 metres within the boundary line at some areas to provide shading green area for the public walkway. This also creates the nice visual impact from the street to the development. A simple plastered and painted wall in random pattern creates a welcome frontage along the street. At the canal side, the designers create a continuity open terrace, which embraced the canal environment. At this area, the residents can relax in the tranquil garden and can enjoy the view of the canal and the old residential compound at the opposite side. This space would also benefit the overall canalscape.

4. Waterscape
The swimming pool is built on top of the parking podium on 5th floor. The given space for the facility is not large enough to serve the large proportion of the project residents. The design approach is

intended to make the space look larger while maintaining the function of the swimming pool. The designers propose to camouflage all the pool functions (i.e. pool terrace, play pool, and spa pool) under the water surface in order to extend the water surface visually. One of the design characters of this pool is the series of floating planters which sunken below the water level. These planters help create the feeling of swimming amongst swamp atmosphere.

5. Microclimate and Planting

Since the building mass dominates the major spaces of the project, leaving the narrow strips along the northeast and southwest sides. Additionally, this gigantic building resulted in the blockage of the natural ventilation that should be flowing from the canal to the front garden. To deal with this problem, the semi-outdoor terrace is introduced to connect both areas together, allowing the wind to flow more continuously and creating the channeling of vista to the canal scenery.

The concept of plant selection which is based upon the function of each specific area should match the canal ecology as well. At the front garden where the lobby and parking lots are located, the plant selection at this area must help absorb pollution effectively, provide shade, and form the space of the arrival court.

2. Raised flower bed
3-4. Detail of the flower bed

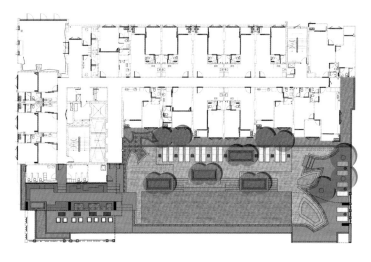

Pool plan

5. The design approach is to maintain the continuity of the green area along both sides as much as possible
6. The series of planters at the vertical plane of the building
7. Shadow of the trees on the window
8-9. The swimming pool

BRILLIA OSHIMA KOMATSUGAWA PARK

Location: Tokyo, Japan
Design: Yendo Associates
Photography: EARTHSCAPE
Area: 3,000sqm

The design within the landscape design of the Brillia Oshima Komatsugawa Park creates the ability to "experience a variety of moments": from gazing over the transience of the four seasons as a part of everyday life, to feeling the rhythm of the city on your skin, to sometimes spending personal time surrounded by greenery.

The designers felt that allowing all residents to enjoy the park however they wish, rooted in their own lifestyles, was an important element of hospitality provided by the landscape of this residency, and was something that landscape design should do.

Just as an island is a stage that nurtures a plenitude of life through a diversity of locations and experiences, Brillia Oshima Komatsugawa Park is also home to a diverse sense of "time" that showcases the life here. The "Residential Island" is a stage for peoples' lives, boasting both the sense of luxury of a hotel, and a quality of lifestyle rooted in the region.

The different functions of outdoor space limit the people's behaviours. The ground of the vertical design is very simple, mainly through the ground shop outfit and greening rich visual effect.

Furniture design satisfies the human scale and material selection of enhanced sense of experience. In addition, the lamplight of setting strengthened space also makes the whole outdoor space more warmth.

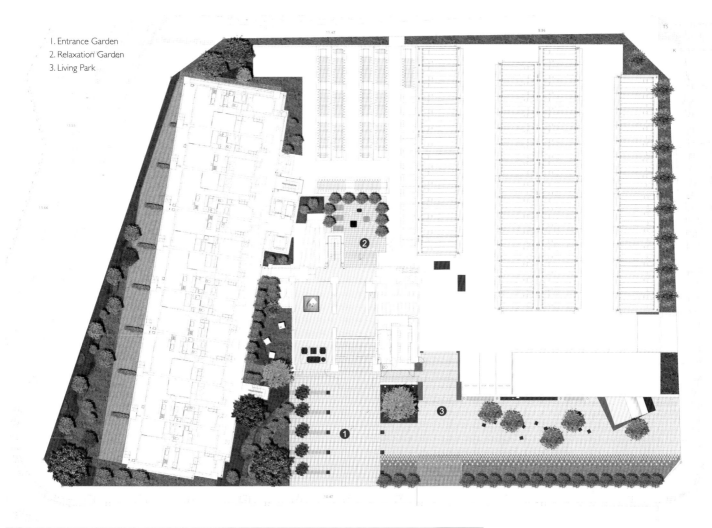

1. Entrance Garden
2. Relaxation Garden
3. Living Park

Master plan

1. Brillia Oshima Komatsugawa Park
2. Concise pavement and the green plants
3. The seats for residents
4. Night view of the community

5. The tree bed
6. Outside furniture
7. The lamplight of setting

SUMMER PLACE

Location: Penang, Malaysia
Design: LandArt Design Sdn Bhd
Photography: LandArt Design Sdn Bhd
Area: 25,293sqm
Award: Malaysia Landscape Architecture
(ILAM) Awards 2011

Sitting on 6.25 acres, off Jelutong Expressway, Summer Place is a waterfront condominium located at the northern end of the newly developed, residential area of Bandar Sri Pinang in Georgetown, Penang. A panoramic view of the sea including the Penang Bridge, the promenade and easy access to town and the bridge, helped to project the Summer Place as a seaside holiday retreat. It consists of three towers which houses more than 500 units, the upper medium cost condominium provides a full range of amenities and facilities for the pleasure and convenience of its residents. Even though this scheme comes equipped with an automation system, in order to fully complement the condo facilities, the landscape design has to be the forefront element. At the end of the day, the residents will be benefit from this comprehensive package which comes with an alluring environment.

The whole idea is about creating a bold, contemporary and vibrant garden to suit the needs of a high density, vertical living community. Besides simplicity in the appearance of the landscape, the innovative design will offset the image of this formerly, reclaimed land. This geographically sea fronting advantage should be taken into consideration when designing and transforming the landscape features. A crucial element that needs to be weaved into this concept is functionality. This is about how the amenities featured in the landscape design are able to benefit this particular community, allowing them to interact within the underlying concept of inclusion and unity in sustaining this waterfront community.

This is a contemporary, tropical garden which lies within a shrouded sanctuary.

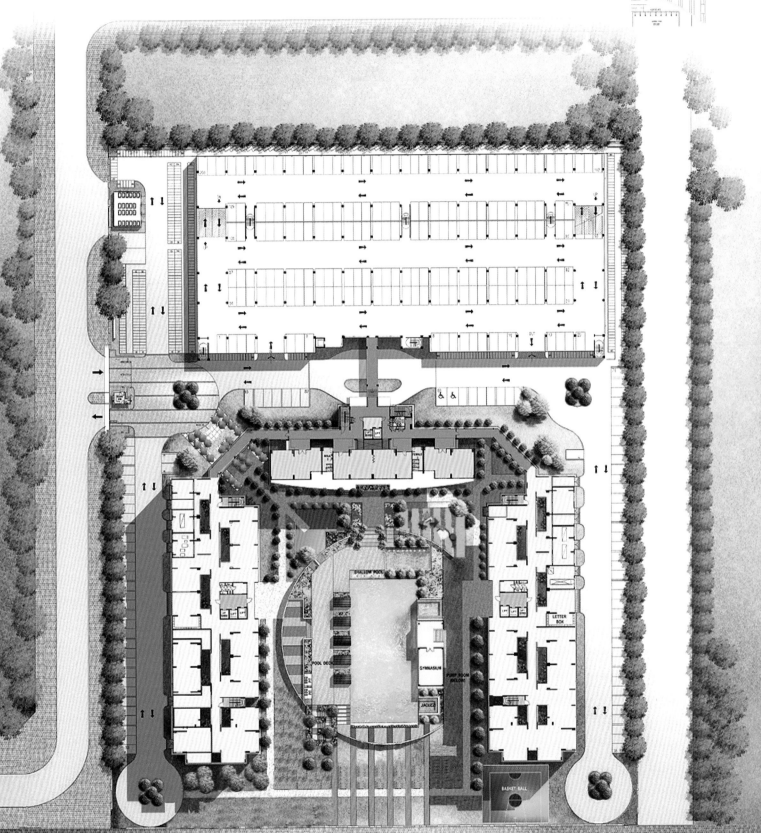

Master plan

The architectural planning creates a concentrated landscaped area which comprised three tower blocks. Formerly, a dumping site, 1.2 metres of soil was removed and replaced with new topsoil in order to overcome the acidic soil conditions. As this project is about creating a holiday seaside retreat with summer activities, the water elements has been adopted as the main theme to complement the sea view context.

The centralised contemporary garden forms a gigantic circle on the plan view to break the rigidity of the designated landscaped area. This circular shape is intended to tangibly portray a sense of inclusion, unity and togetherness in the overall design. Meanwhile, access to the blocks is highlighted with parallel alternate colours. Each lining feature paving traversed from each lift lobby, where 1.5 metre wide walk ways frame the circular garden. This pattern extends to the softscape as well as the Ophiopogon jaburan flanked by its alternate, variegated species.

1. Bird view of this waterfront condominium

5

This subtly raised one metre high pool deck elevated the view from the pool outwards to the sea shore. The elevated garden consists of the following amenities: main infinity pool, wading pool, timber deck cabanas, pavilion with indoor gym and Jacuzzis. Again, the parallel line pattern has been fabricated, vertically with stainless steel standing together with orangy broken mosaic water spout panels. The water element persists with water flowing to the edge of the 40 metre long, rippling infinity pool.

2. The appearance of the landscape is simple
3-4. The featured pavement
5. The tropical garden lies within a shrouded sanctuary

6. Bold, contemporary and vibrant residential garden
7. Main infinity pool
8. The water element persists with water flowing to the edge of the 40 metre long, rippling infinity pool
9-10. The playground

XIN TIAN 40°N RESIDENTIAL DEVELOPMENT

Location: Beijing, China
Completion: 2012
Design: HASSELL
Photography: Yang Qitao
Area: 256,000sqm

40°N is a 13.8ha residential development located in the Chaoyang District of Beijing. HASSELL's design included the landscape design of the residential area as well as an 11.8ha adjacent public park. The name of the project, 40°N not only refers to the latitudinal location of the site, but also refers to the metaphorical relationship between space and time. Just as movement through space can bring about a diverse range of experiences, the landscape can convey a variety of impressions through its colour, shape and form. The HASSELL scheme sought to create opportunities for different experiences in the landscape – for moments of pause and for moments of passing.

A landscape spine runs diagonally across the site, linking together 5 thematic residential gardens that are formed by the staggered arrangement of residential tower blocks. Each garden conveys a different set of experiences, to either pass through or to stay. Vertical elements such as timber trellises, feature walls, pergolas, and allees of trees act to define each space. The landscape form is a juxtaposition of square and rounded elements – created by the rectilinear form of the buildings and the elliptical form of garden islands. Water is introduced throughout the site – enhancing a rich sensory experience of sound, touch and smell.

Since the project is located in Beijing, a city suffers from water shortage and with strict restriction on water consumption; effective use of water is also a focus of the project. In the long run, this unique design is not only environment-friendly, but also saves large amount of water for the residents.

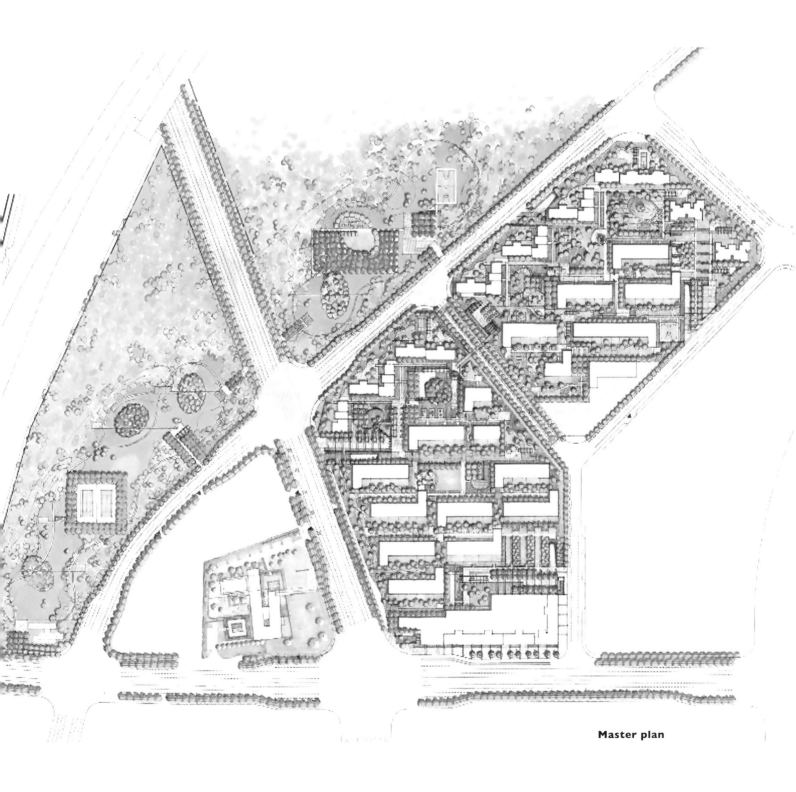

Master plan

1. The playground
2. The landscape form is a juxtaposition of square and rounded elements
3-4. The design seeks to create opportunities for different experiences in the landscape – for moments of pause and for moments of passing

5. Shelter
6-8. The water feature
9-10. The pavement
11. The tree plaza

PROVINCE – PORTLAND, ZHENGZHOU

Location: Zhengzhou, China
Completion: 2013
Design: Horizon & Atmosphere Landscape Co.
Photography: duo-image associates
Area: 39,473sqm

Filling the Community with Youth

"Youth" stands for joy, fashion and vitality. In the landscape design of Portland Residential Project, Zhengzhou, the designers take "Youth's Vital Community" as the vision. The youth is a generation full of vigour and spirits and their community should also correspond to their characters. Therefore, the designers fill this community with joy, fashion and vitality and wish it become a unique youth community, which full of youthful feelings, passion and enthusiasm.

The combination of colours, patterns and materials provide the space with charming atmosphere. As residents walk, chat, exercise, play and enjoy views, they will indulge in pleasure and reluctant to leave.

The youth always possess a beautiful vision towards the future. Thus, with the focus on rich landscape colours and line variety, the designers also make efforts to enrich community activities and complete various supporting facilities. They even simulate activity schedule and participating groups of each area and attempt to experience the participants' feelings. The community also provides an exclusive kindergarten and thoughtful property services. Moreover, the designers further suggest the developer to transform the sales centre into an art centre which gathers children library, gym and art gallery after the housing units are sold out. They believe this measure will surely promote the community's art and cultural qualities.

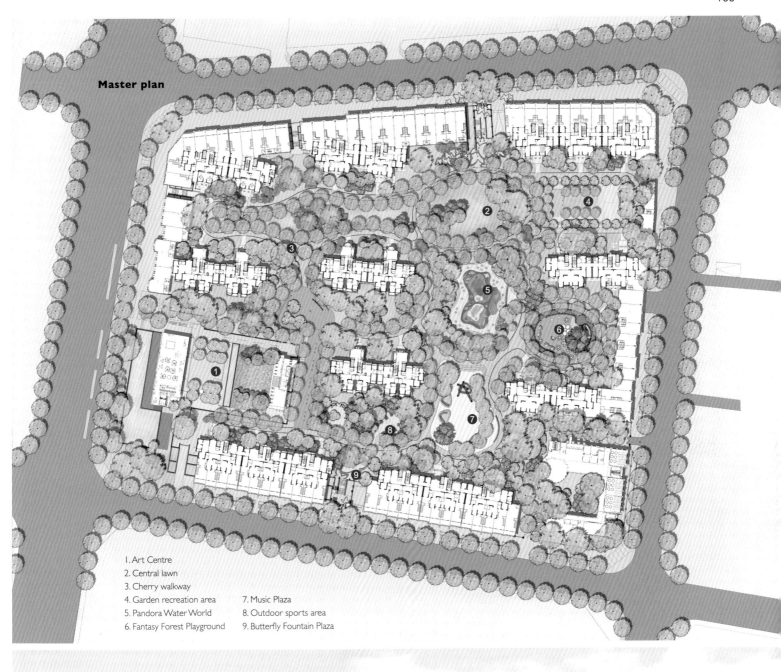

Master plan

1. Art Centre
2. Central lawn
3. Cherry walkway
4. Garden recreation area   7. Music Plaza
5. Pandora Water World   8. Outdoor sports area
6. Fantasy Forest Playground   9. Butterfly Fountain Plaza

Elevation

1. The sight starts from the entry sign extended to the green lawn, tree, water feature and the architecture
2. The plaza
3. Butterfly Fountain Plaza

3

4

4. Bird eye view of the Music Art Plaza
5. Olympic Plaza
6. The Music Art Plaza – sculpture that performs the dialogue between art and space

7. Bird eye view of the Fantasy Forest Playground
8. Overall view of the Fantasy Forest – more extended discovery and experiences
9. Pandora Water World
10. The Fantasy Forest – creating the entertainment, sense of touch and perception into a whole

ORIENTAL BLESSING

Location: Hangzhou, China
Completion: 2013
Principle designer: Li Baozhang
Associate designer: Feng Zhe, Huang Wenchang, Wu Di, Ma Wei, Yuan Li, Zhu Shuang, Zhao Qiong, Yang Zhen, Liu Tongchao, Li Dinghong
Photography: Zhang Qianxi
Area: 110,000sqm

The project makes the most of the poetic essence of contemporary landscape in Hangzhou. The real intention of landscape designers is to emphasise "implication of image", which completes the design through materialised inner feeling, philosophic experience and association with unique images. The poetic picture drawn with a pine tree, several lush shrubs and a few flowers expresses an indescribable wonderful feeling.

The quality and artistic landscape design in Hangzhou is based on the city's extensive and profound cultural roots. On one hand, Taoist idea of "Human beings are a manifestation of the earth; the earth, a manifestation of the physical universe; the physical universe, a manifestation of Infinity; Infinity, the potential of all things" generates the principles of Chinese classic landscape design. On the other hand, the Zen idea of "Green bamboos are embodiment of truth and law, while yellow flowers are wisdom" provides theoretic support for "much in little" design of classic landscape.

By reference to local landscape concept in Hangzhou, the designers reinterpret it in contemporary methods to create a modern landscape with fresh air, warm sunshine, flowing stream and forest-like greenery. The waterfall and rockery define the entrance while exclusive loop home-entry design indicates the nobility. The surrounding sky level connects three high-rise units like a covered verandah. The view lobby juxtaposes with feature pavilion outside and the secluded paths link the exterior landscape with interior sky level. The ups and downs of rockery reinforce the depth of the garden; the rich plantings convey a natural and elegant lifestyle;

Master plan

1. The most of the poetic essence of contemporary landscape in Hangzhou
2. Exclusive loop home-entry design indicates the nobility

2

the beautiful landscape provides visitors and residents carefree and content feelings.

In general, the implementation of Oriental Blessing project is excellent. Especially the landscape construction highly implements the design intention. The original landscape concept is to build a retreat for urban residents to live with nature and community harmoniously. Living with family in an environment surrounded by landscape is the ideal living state of the Chinese. The landscape design of Oriental Blessing realises this result to a maximum degree. The waterfall and garden at the entrance change from winding paths to openness. The housing units are faced with delicate rockery and water features and enjoy a lush greenery view. From the elaborately stacked hills, undulating paths to rich plantings, the landscape construction constantly strives for excellence, which shows delicacy and leisure lifestyle in landscape details.

3. The rockery at the entrance area
4. Garden pavilion
5. The waterfall at the entrance area

6

213

6. The rich plantings
7-8. The secluded paths

LAKE VIEW SETTLEMENTS, SHAOXING

Location: Shaoxing, China
Completion: 2014
Design: SED Landscape Architects Co.,LTD.
Photography: SED Landscape Architects Co.,LTD.
Area: 44,845sqm

The designers divide the whole project into two areas: South Area and North Area according to their programmes. North Area focuses on functionality and forms a fully functional and generous space effect. South Area is mainly created through natural forms. Plantings and various landscape feature spaces express a delicate and natural atmosphere.

In the display area, the designers respond to the buildings' Neo-Asian style and create a unique landscape feeling through hierarchy of planting, pierced feature wall, sunshine lawn, reflection pool and gravel landscape, etc. Adjacent to the waterfront landscape, the project provides residents a resort-style living space with combination of waterfront lifestyle and new interpretation of Chinese traditional garden.

Main Nodes Design
Entrance Plaza and Front Plaza of Clubhouse: The clean and quiet entrance plaza leads people to the clubhouse with a bluestone paved path flanked by rows of bamboos. A reflection pool responds to the buildings' facades and the aquatic plants pat the water surface with breeze. Gravel strips spread in reflection pool, paths and lawn. Light and shadow play an interesting effect through the pierced feature wall to the well-paved ground.

Sunshine Lawn and Parking Lot: The whole parking lot is enclosed by lush greenery in various heights. Hidden in plants, the parking lot enjoys an ecological and natural environment. The sunshine lawn surrounded by trees and shrubs brings a hint of leisure for the whole space. Gravel paths meander in the bamboo grove and are spotted through sunshine and shadows. Walking in the grove aimlessly, one could enjoy a relaxed feeling.

Waterfront Landscape: The riverway separates the sales centre and the project. A wooden deck links the two sides, which is accented by weeping willows along the river. Seen from the clubhouse to the opposite side, the buildings in layered

Master plan

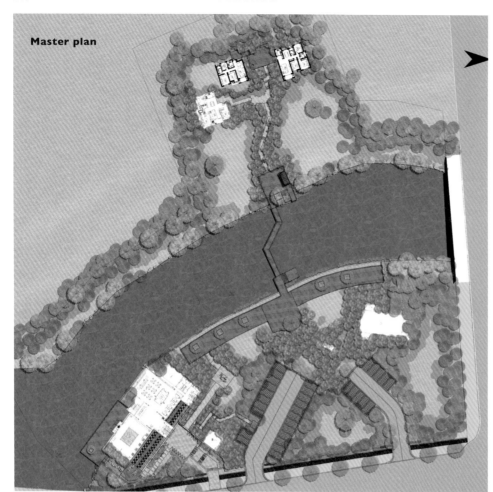

planting express a unique spatial feeling. With clusters of aquatic plants spreading along the river, the waterfront provides a fresh and natural atmosphere.

Model Housing Display Area: Walking through the wooden deck, one will enjoy a panoramic view of the lake. In this display area, one is fully immersed in a beautiful mood. Lake View Settlements provide residents an elegant lifestyle with lush greenery and natural feeling.

217

1. A delicate and natural atmosphere
2. The clean and quiet entrance plaza
3. A bluestone paved path flanked by rows of bamboos
4. Layered planting

5. The path with green plants and flowers
6. The architecture on the opposite site of the river
7. The stairs on the slope
8. The water feature in the model housing display area
9. Night view of the water feature

ZHONGZHOU CENTRAL PARK, SHENZHEN

Location: Shenzhen, China
Completion: 2014
Design: SED Landscape Architects Co.,LTD.
Photography: SED Landscape Architects Co.,LTD.
Area: 90,800 sqm

Zhongzhou Central Park is one of the "Central Parks" produced by Zhongzhou Estate and located in 26th zone of Bao'an district with an area of more than 90,000 square metres covering A, B and C districts. District A and B are high-grade residence while C is mainly for the comprehension of commercial and offices which takes up 510,000 square metres for the buildings. Being surrounded by the traffic nets and across from the park, it has a great geographical advantage.

Confronting both the urban development and the vintage monument, the project chose Art Deco to express this sort of cultural shock to reveal the historical sediment and natural treasure. Art Deco originates from France between the artists and the nobles who urged to show their life style and avant-garde attitude, which is kind of similar with those nowadays. That is also the most charming part of the Art Deco. The project pays attention on the texture and gloss of the materials with the stereotype from the geometric art symbols in Art Deco to create special aesthetics ambience. Featured sculptures of elegance together with the brief space arrangement offer a character landscape design.

Adorned with the Nobleness and Graceful Quality

District A, being abounded by Art Deco feelings, lies in the northwest part with an area of 40,000 square metres in total. Drained from the natural source, the inner water system is separates into two parts respectively as the pool and lake for the golf island by the axis. The landscape spots are joined by elegant line smoothly. Open leisure space, semi-open green area and private garden form an eco-system in the district. Innovation ideas has been used to combine the SPA resort, vertical diversity and the landscape together without any deliberation, expressing the grace at the same time.

Diamond Dynasty, the grand entrance, manages the front garden and meanwhile is the important mark of the project. Its modern fashioned details, gorgeously decorated, show a ceremony feeling in royalty naturally. Ordered design makes people feel slowing down by the gentle elegance.

1

2

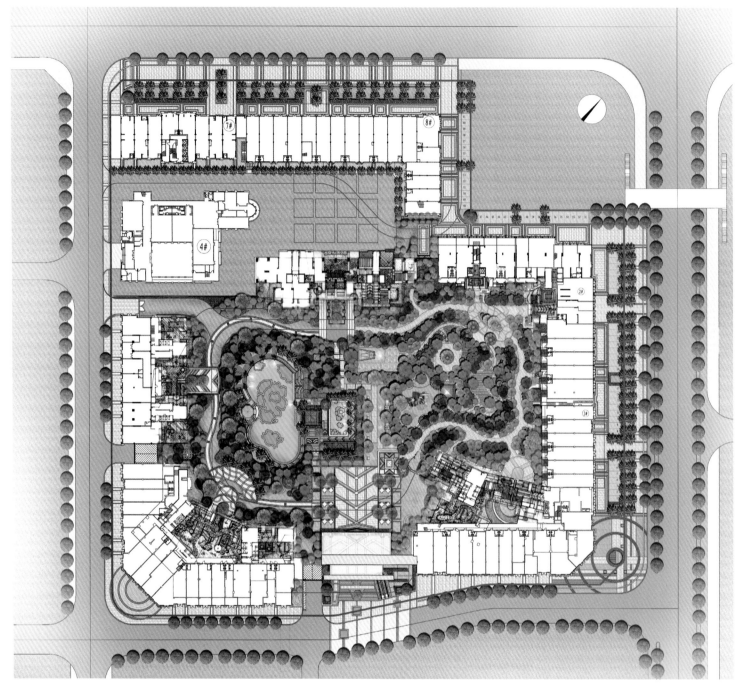

Master plan

Cuishan court section

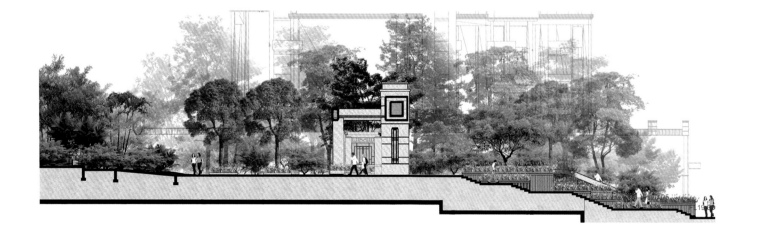

1-2. Bird eye view of the community
3. The entrance
4. Night view of the community landscape

Passing through the Diamond Dynasty, a plaza shows up named after the sun that is the typical sign of reign's power and sparkling life. The real luxury from the nobleness brings the residents a high end identity and the construction of the pretty platform and the party square is to highlight and fit it.

The "Time Rose Pool", moreover, lets people fully relaxed in the peaceful mood. The rose pattern dose not mean the beauty of this flower only but the joy, the entertainment and the blooming life representing the memory of time and lasts forever, becoming the "rose of time".

Following the function parts the pool is divided into the children's part and the adults' part. The whole pool is managed in close-end way and raised up 750mm. The fitting room takes use of the underground space accompanied with a hotel scale of the SPA resort and the bathrooms.

The Wizard of Oz is a roof garden within which the plants rise layer by layer, alleviating the depression feeling brought by the high-rise buildings and creating a sense of romantic with interest. The architecture fits the city figure and shows the expanding and rich room, the surrounding source is under proper use with protection, everyone can feel the friendly

5

atmosphere and attached to their homeland…these are what we all expect.

Geomantic Vegetation Arrangement

The vegetation design not only makes the living circumstance comfortable and delicate but also takes care of the variety of the space to make it feel more natural flowing. The shape-followed plants layout gives a rhythm. According to the geomantic sayings ever green trees are priority in the main entrance with the front scene consisted of broadleaf plants covering the whole Diamond Dynasty, explaining the traditional auspicious implies. Linkage and screen are set to complete the whole geomantic pattern as well.

Exalted Residential Impression Made by Sculptures

Eagle-shaped sculpture is taken in use as a mark of alien aroma. Art Deco was populated in USA especially its heart city, New York. As the result their bird of union, eagle, has a unique representation. Metalised bronze surface and its abstract looking with mechanical aesthetics show a kind of distance exalted feeling.

Art Details in Pavements

Pavements are almost in warm colour with Art Deco style showing the texture and the sheen. Intense contrast, geometric figures and pure colour mixed by metal feelings give a splendid visual impact.

Leimeng lake garden sections

5. The path with green plantings
6. The water feature
7. Night view of the water feture

8. The fountain nozzle
9. The sculpture
10. The shelter
11. The playground

• *Low-rise
villa
landscape*

CHELONA LANDSCAPE

Location: Prachuap khiri khan,Thainland
Completion: 2013
Design: Wannaporn Suwannatrai
(Openbox Company Limited)
Photography: Wison Tungthunya
Area: 2,740sqm

OPNBX was approached by Sansiri to propose landscape design for a beachfront condominium in Huahin. Developed to be a weekend home, Chelona has been assigned to be resemblance of a relaxing, little town in Greece. In close collaboration with Agalio Studio, the design architect of the project, architecture and landscape concept has merged seamlessly into one.

The site is a typical beachfront formation with a narrow frontage facing the beach and very long strip stretching over ten times the width to connect to the access road. The site was mainly covered in sand. One third of the land has been occupied by fully grown existing trees. All of them are local and have withstood sea wind for a long time and have turned into sculpture forms.

Typically for a long site with a narrow side facing the beach, only a few units have the direct sea view. The rest of the units would have to rely on variety of intense landscape creation to become the views. Even with limited palette of white to light colour hardscape, water feature and natural plant colours, variation of experience could still be created, based on differences of directions, lines, curves and height.

Aside from the obvious thematic design, the most important task is to keep as many of the existing trees as possible. OPNBX team has begun by documenting all trees, going through selection process, and propose tree saving features in design: such as
• Adjusting the design to fit the existing tree locations, not the other way around. In a few extreme cases, positions of buildings are adjusted to fit in among the existing trees;
• Leaving lots of space around existing balls;
• Hiring a specialist to be on board since day one of construction;
• All these have to be done without losing the efficiency of the salable.

In this case, the designers considered themselves very successful in saving the trees and they return the favour by making the project feel very "lush" and "alive" since the first day of opening.

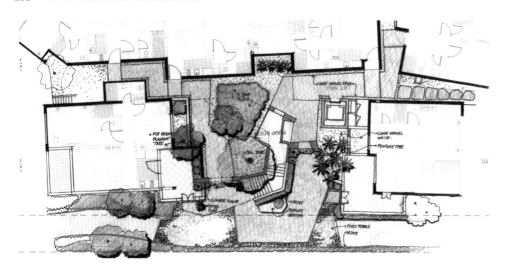

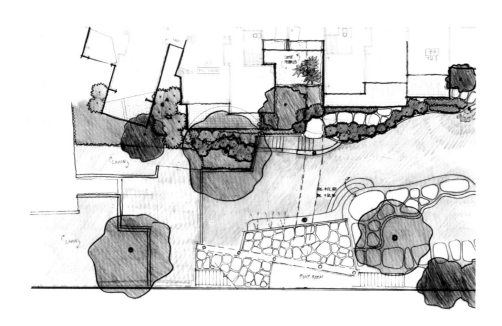

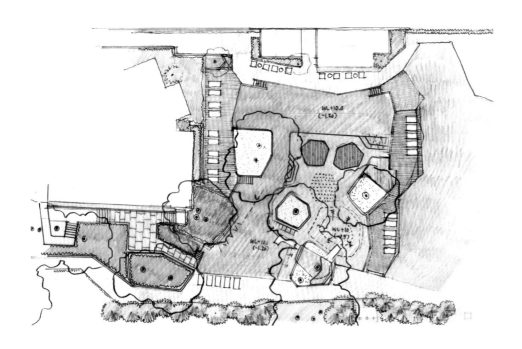

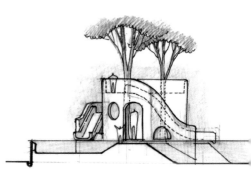

1. Architecture and landscape concept has merged seamlessly into one
2. A narrow frontage facing the beach
2. The slide for children

4

4. The water feature and the lush green plants
5. The trees are local and have withstood sea wind for a long time and have turned into sculpture forms
6. Variety of intense landscape creation
7. The clear water

INDOCHINA VILLAS SAIGON

Location: Ho Chi Minh City, Vietnam
Completion: 2014
Design: ONE landscape
Photography: Jason Findley, Aaron
Joel Santos
Area: 80,000sqm
Plant information: Plumeria species,
Terminalia mantaly "Variegata", Delonix regia

Developed by Vietnam's premier real estate company INDOCHINA LAND, boutique waterfront residential project in Ho Chi Minh City is an upcoming high-end villa development of 8 ha. Inspired by the linearity of the vast paddy fields that marks Vietnam's dramatic landscape, the design includes a series of vibrant community spaces that are interconnected through a safe and secure public realm based on "access for all" philosophy. The community spaces – a linear waterfront park, community swimming pool plaza, neighbourhood park and children's play park are all linked together with the unifying geometrical abstraction of rice grain, thus an extension of the paddy fields concept.

This villa experience begins with the entry statement at its frontage to the main road. Inspired by the rice pattern the boundary wall is unique in creating a strong identity and character. The boundary wall further merges with the art wall – the most important feature of the entry experience. The wall with its sculpted pattern with deep shadows changes character in the evening when the light box installed behind the wall softly glows to create a dramatic statement.

The rice inspired pattern unifies and manifests itself in a series of scales throughout the project especially in the community pool area located just after the entrance. Designed as the key gathering place, this area visually connects the adjacent lake with its infinity swimming pool featuring a linear deck canopy structure. With its rich patterned panels as both horizontal and vertical support elements it is an elegant structure of sculptural qualities. A shaded corridor of similar design character connects the Tai Chi Plaza with the waterfront BBQ deck and features children's water fountain. Inspired by the lotus and conceived as a feature play fountain the sculptural installation is more an artwork than a water feature. Dramatic lighting in this area highlights the sculptural elements and brings a boutique resort feel to the development.

1. Night view of Eden
2. The entrance
3. The wall with its sculpted pattern with deep shadows changes character in the evening
4. Clean and simple landscape

Master plan

1. Night view of Eden
2. The entrance
3. The wall with its sculpted pattern with deep shadows changes character in the evening
4. Clean and simple landscape

Further down the development is the neighbourhood park, the other key park space within the project. Conceived as green oasis and also accessed from the linear waterfront park, it is a space with many unique features. The shape and pattern inspired by the geometrical abstraction of the rice grain finds new forms, the most common being the feature screen. Set against lush planting the screens create a new setting within this park. A series of platforms with linear benches act as places for relaxation and contemplation. The park also contains a central floating

canopy hovering among the tree layer, its elegant floating plane in complete contrast to the tree foliage. Supported by a series of slender metal columns its sculptural quality is further enhanced by a series of cutouts in shapes of the pattern, not only to reduce load but also invite exciting play of shadows on the ground. A series of stepping stones on the lawn in the same geometric shape adds unity to the theme and creates the illusion of the pavilion cutouts being are mere subtractions only to appear on the ground as stepping stones. A series of sculptural seats as extrusions of the geometric shape appear among the greenery as contrast against the backdrop of lush foliage. Lighting further creates drama in highlighting these key landscape features within the park.

5. The pavilion
6. Set against lush planting the screens create a new setting within this park
7. The infinity swimming pool featuring a linear deck canopy structure
8. The pavement
9. A series of platforms with linear benches act as places for relaxation and contemplation

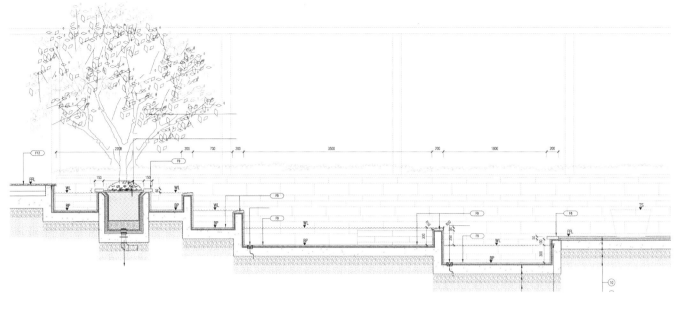

Sections

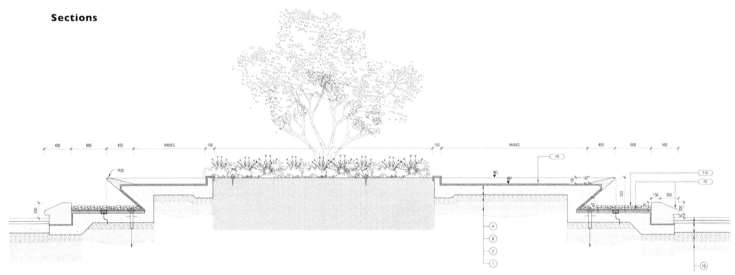

ONE's approach of integrating art and culture in this project creates a unique landscape to be enjoyed both the residents and its visitors, making EDEN a landmark development of Ho Chi Minh City and creating a new benching in resort style city living.

10. Water feature
11. Water cascade
12. Central floating canopy
13. Inspired by the lotus and conceived as a feature play fountain the sculptural installation

MARICOLLE

Location: Fukuoka, Japan
Design: wa-so design
Photography: Kazufumi Nakamura
Area: point A: 590.1sqm, point B: 197.3sqm
point C: 83.4sqm

This is a refurbishment project, with the garden and interior and exterior of wedding facilities located at seaside in Kokura city. It was requested to design not only beautiful but also as a place that could take a wedding party. We considered to create an extraordinary memorable and enjoyable space and scenery, therefore first of all, we assigned two concepts: "waterfront resort" and "highland resort". Existed grass area is expanded as a refurbishment area according to place together a part of parking, and a new garden taking a leading part of pool is made there. There are a bridge and an island covered with wooden deck as a stage for leading couple in ceremony. The sidewall of the pool is sloped to make the most of water lights efficiently and it makes sense for structure as well. Some water fountain nozzles are set up inline, hence they are possible to make a water wall. It is possible to control water height freely from a counter that was arranged inside area. There are the special spaces surrounded by plants on the other side, and wooden deck and tiled space are secured for the participants in ceremony as much as possible. On the other side, with the trees in wooden deck, it seems to be in a small forest when you participate in the party. We considered to use evergreen trees mainly for instance Fraxinus griffithii because the facility is open all the year round. Not only are there some exterior sofas, a projector and sound system are also furnished in this hall in addition.

1-2. The featured swimming pool
3. The entrance area is mainly white and green
4. Exterior sofa for relaxing

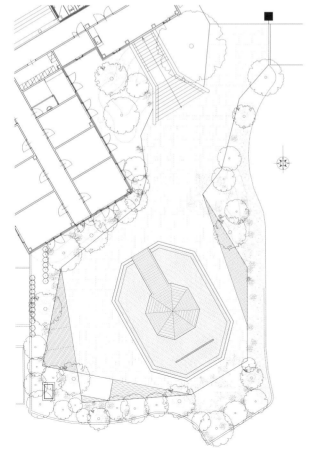

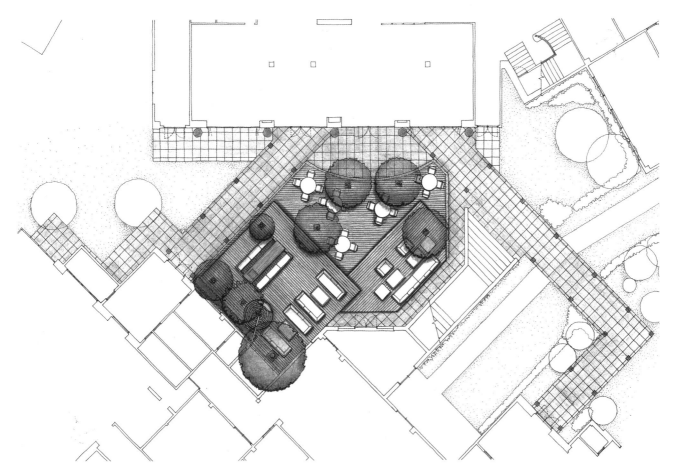

5. Night view of the landscape
6-7. lighting detail
8. Evergreen trees mainly for instance Fraxinus
griffithii are used most
9. The pavement detail

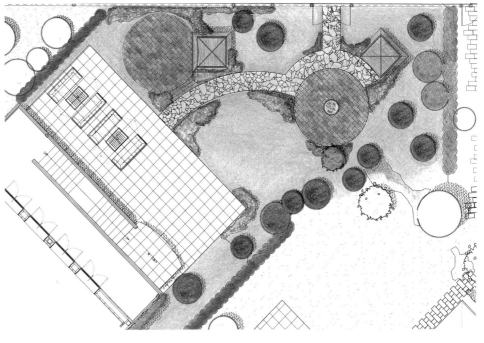

MANGROVE PARK AND NEWPORT QUAYS STAGE 1

Location: Ethelton, Australia
Design: Taylor Cullity Lethlean
Photography: Ben Wrigley
Area: 7,000sqm

The redevelopment of the Port Adelaide inner harbour is one of South Australia's largest and most significant urban development projects. Taylor Cullity Lethlean was engaged by the Brookfield Multiplex – Urban Construct joint venture to undertake urban and landscape design for the first stage including the regeneration of the adjacent portions of Mangrove Park. Through close collaboration with Cox Architects, significant changes were made to the road treatments removing kerbs and creating a more pedestrian friendly environment.

Working within the constraints of the predetermined built form planning, Taylor Cullity Lethlean created a series of landscaped spaces of great variety and high amenity. The scope of services included the design of all exterior spaces including the waterfront promenade, outdoor structures and furniture, decking, paving and planting. Working within a tight budgetary framework, care was taken to add detail to furniture and structures wherever possible. Similarly, planting was selected to add patterning, colour and spatial definition to the landscape.

Soil conditions on the site are particularly difficult with the entire development constructed over remediated soils. Taylor Cullity Lethlean worked closely with geotechnical and civil engineers, soil scientists and arborists to develop a soil profile which met the stringent remediation requirements while providing a suitable growing medium for plants. The thriving plantings which have become a feature of the development are testament to the successful resolution of the extremely difficult site soil challenges.

In Mangrove Park at the southern end of the development, extensive soil amelioration and the planting of 37,000 indigenous plants has successfully rehabilitated this formerly degraded section of the park. Consultation with the adjacent school ensures that the park is a venue for their environmental education programs.

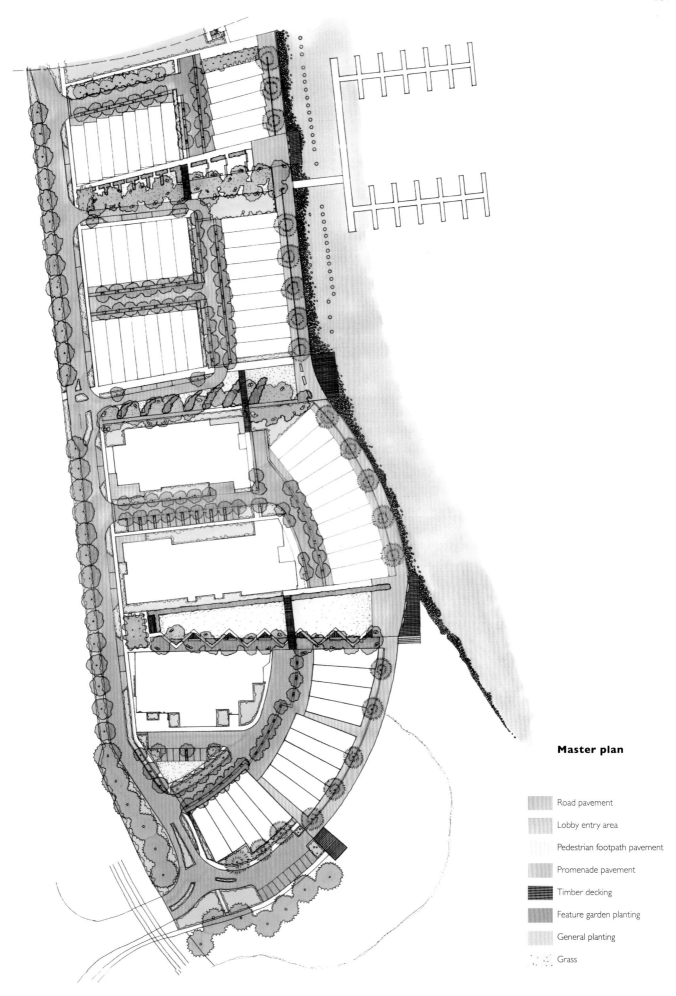

Master plan

Road pavement

Lobby entry area

Pedestrian footpath pavement

Promenade pavement

Timber decking

Feature garden planting

General planting

Grass

The first stage of Newport Quays provides residents and the general public with a readable hierarchy of private, communal and public spaces which contribute to the landscape amenity of the local neighbourhood and broader region. The rehabilitation of Mangrove Park and the design and construction of the first stage of the waterfront promenade with its associated decks, shelters and gathering spaces are particularly important aspects of the project for the enjoyment of the wider community.

Design of the residential landscape of the Newport Quays development involved an intensive collaboration with site architects and civil engineers to substantially influence the road character between residential buildings, including deletion of kerbs and adoption of centre drainage. Also, pavement selection and planting design were carefully undertaken with detailed review and consultation with all relevant parties. Particularly successful has been the planting selection to create a thriving landscape in dry coastal conditions in very limited soil volume.

The Newport Quays development is one of few examples in South Australia of intensively landscaped medium density housing and apartment developments in which a landscape architectural lead approach was taken to all outdoor spaces. The result has been a clear concept which expresses a hierarchy of public, semi-public and private spaces with public waterfront promenade and roadways, public/communal parkland wedges between building blocks, and private courts for townhouses.

The Newport Quays Stage 1 and Mangrove Park designs involved two major site specific environmental undertakings. The whole Stage 1 development was undertaken on a previously industrial brown-field site with considerable soil contamination. Extensive and thorough soil remediation was undertaken to allow residential development to occur. This involved intensive collaboration with engineers

1. A series of landscaped spaces of great variety and high amenity
2. The thriving plantings which have become a feature of the development
3. The ornamental trees in front of the building

and scientists by the landscape architect to create a suitable growing environment for a successful landscape.

The second major undertaking was the rehabilitation and revegetation of a large portion of the Mangrove Park site. This site included a remnant stand of indigenous mangrove forest and associated samphire plant communities. The planting of over 37,000 indigenous plants has vastly improved and ensured the survival of the mangroves and samphire marshes and general biodiversity of this site on the Port River.

255

4. Particularly successful has been the planting selection to create a thriving landscape in dry coastal conditions in very limited soil volume
5. Night view of the community landscape
6. Planting was selected to add patterning, colour and spatial definition to the landscape
7. Care was taken to add detail to furniture and structures wherever possible

SOMMETS-SUR-LE-FLEUVE

Location: Montréal, Canada
Design: Williams Asselin Ackaoui & Associates Inc
Photography: Vincent Asselin
Area: 75,000sqm

The "Sommets-sur-le-Fleuve" project is a landscape design for a newly built prestigious apartment tower complex. Located on the shores of Nuns' Island, a small "green" island across the river from the Island of Montreal, the apartment towers are blessed with a sublime view over the St. Lawrence River, and the city of Montreal and its downtown.

A succession of four typologies of gardens takes us on a trip through pedestrian and bicycle paths, a pagoda band shelter, a sculpture garden and a formal square.

Lush planting, floral displays, butterfly gardens, tree-lined thoroughfare and formal gardens garnish and add value to the already beautiful site; they also embellish the residential complex, as well as offer a more agreeable view from the floors up, to the gardens at grade.

Plant Information
Trees: Amelanchier canadensis, Acer ginnala, Gleditsia triacanthos "Shademaster", Prunus serotina, Syringa reticulata "Ivory Silk", Thuja occidentalis "Fastigiata"

Shrubs: Actinidia kolomikta, Amelanchier canadensis "Balerina", Aronia melanocarpa "Vinking", Diervilla lonicera, Eonymus alatus "Compactus", Humulus lupulus, Hydrangea paniculata "Unique"

Perennials: Alchemilla mollis, Ajuga reptans 'Catlin's Giant', Aruncus dioicus 'Sylvestris', Calamagrostis x 'Karl Foster', Calamagrostis brachytricha, Cerastium tomentosum, Geranium sanguineum, Hemerocallis 'Joan Senior'

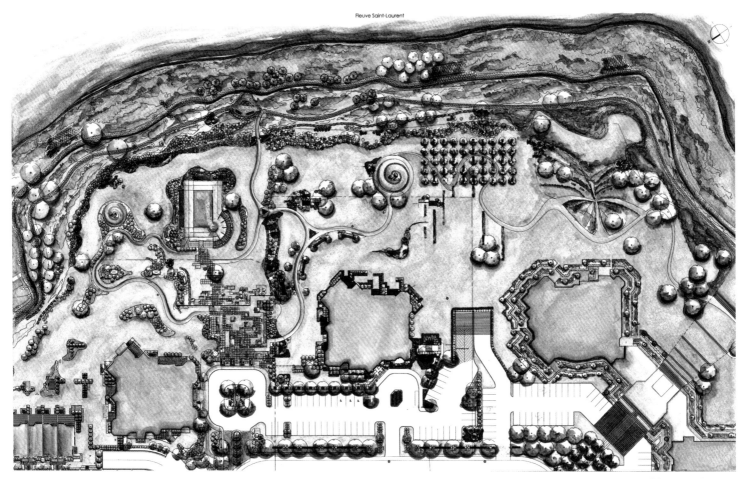

Fleuve Saint-Laurent

Master plan

1. The swimming pool in the community garden
2. The green lawn
3. The lush planting

1. Quarry rock with flat faces +-1 cubic metre, grey
2. Geotextile
3. Potting soil lawn
4. Crushed stone 20 mm net
5. Compacted foundation

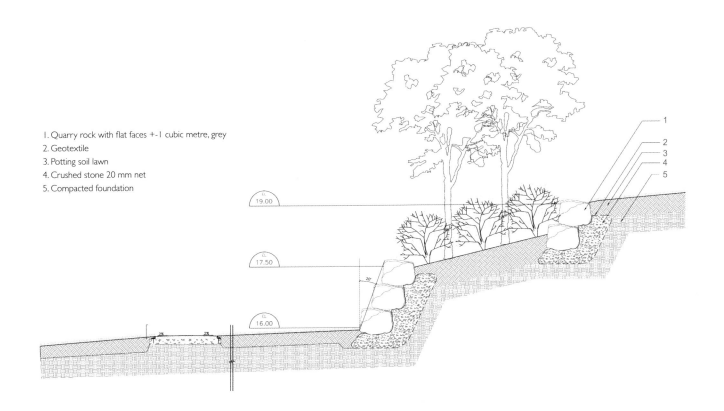

4. Formal gardens
5. Floral displays
6-7. Garden landscape brings a more agree-able view

PROVINCE – ROYAL GARDEN, ZHENGZHOU

Location: Zhengzhou, China
Completion: 2012
Design: Horizon & Atmosphere Landscape Co.
Photography: duo-image associates
Area: 92,205sqm

To Enjoy Considerate and Warm Services

Throughout this over 9,000-square-metre site, each corner and each scene are refined to its best. Focused on atmosphere making, the space is simple yet elegant. It combines different pleasant dimensions into various art spaces. Take the hotel-style main entrance in the east of the site for example. The black and white ground tiles in diamond and repeated sequences reinforce the striking expression of entrance. Without paying any attention, you are already at home. Luxury and elegance, combined with visual art, raise the entrance space into a higher level. For inhabitants, returning home is an enjoyment with considerate hotel-like services, warm home and happiness of the whole community.

To Feel Walking Space

The space is arranged in multiple layers and rhythms. The whole space unfolds through the axis from the luxurious entrance, with border trees continuing the scene visually. Completed with broad central lawn and water feature wall, embellished with fragments of sculptures, the space looks artistic and unique. Walking in the project, your steps will be slowed down by the light grey solids and lush plantings. The open space on a distance scene will surprise you as you walk close. Even the murmur of stream will bring you to another dream. Walking in your way home and setting your body and soul free, you will fully enjoy the delight brought by the whole space, just like that says in the movie "Roman Holiday": "either your body or soul must be on the way".

To Taste Life and Art

The wind outside the wall whips through treetops and telling the seasonal changes of "home". The clean grey colour palette, completed with beige buildings, black water features, green sunshine lawn and seasonal plantings, consist a picturesque artistic space with the charms of black, white, grey and green. In this picture, warm afternoon sunshine penetrates the tree leaves and spills on your body. With a bench, a book and a private space, you can taste your "solitude". Otherwise with a pot of tea under the pergola, you and several friends can talk of everything under the sun.

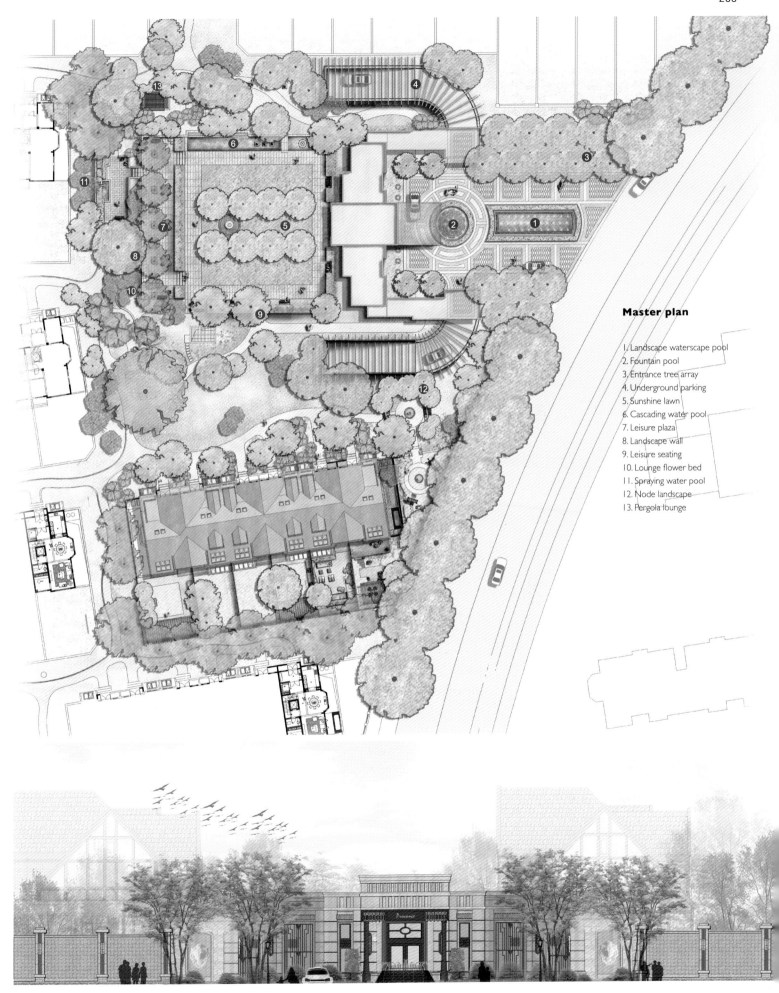

Master plan

1. Landscape waterscape pool
2. Fountain pool
3. Entrance tree array
4. Underground parking
5. Sunshine lawn
6. Cascading water pool
7. Leisure plaza
8. Landscape wall
9. Leisure seating
10. Lounge flower bed
11. Spraying water pool
12. Node landscape
13. Pergola lounge

1. Water feature
2. Sunshine lawn
3. The entrance to the community
4. Night view of the entrance

5-6. Pergola for relaxing
7. Relaxing plaza
8. Waterscape pool

7

8

MOUNTAIN VILLAS OF JINGRUI GROUP, SHAOXING

Location: Shaoxing, Zhejiang
Completion: On going
Design: SED Landscape Architects Co.,LTD.
Photography: SED Landscape Architects Co.,LTD.
Area: 300,000sqm

Situating at Shaoxing, Zhejiang province, the site is part of the Keyan scenic area which proves its convenient traffic, abundant landscape resources and obvious location advantages. A splendid example about the exquisite details treatment and materials application has been set up by the surrounded high quality projects such as Keyan Golf Villas, Keyan Jiahua Fragrant Garden.

Good inheritance to the architecture style is fully shown in the landscape design which demonstrates itself as elegance and simplicity of French Neo-classic but also features as natural and ecological. Harmony of paving materials, colours and architecture materials, as well as the consistency of landscape structures, ornaments and architecture form, enables the integration of landscape and architecture.

The project site is embraced with Dongdan Mountain, with the bluff on its west side. The design brings in the unique concept of "Hidden Mountain – Rock Spa Resort Town" based on the inborn conditions of natural resources, to create a landmark ecological fitness park. The unparalleled regional features and the functions of exercise and fitness endowed by the design, compose the overall connotative tone, distinguishing itself from other projects.

The design tries to introduce a new lifestyle – "Elementary seclusion in mountains, superior seclusion in town" – to express generosity in hidden elements and luxury in low profile. Lush and picturesque landscape creates a high-quality living environment which is similar to a resort. The residents will enjoy a combination of luxurious services and peaceful comforts in this hidden heaven.

As for the unique geological environment of Dongdan Mountain, the designers make use of the topography and retain the existing vegetation, creating a mountainous club landscape and a natural living park for fitness. Through terrain transformation, the designers solve the difference of water level. They use terraced turf slope and rock band to treat the existing riverway and artificial brook, creating a hydrophilic space with consideration of standard flood level.

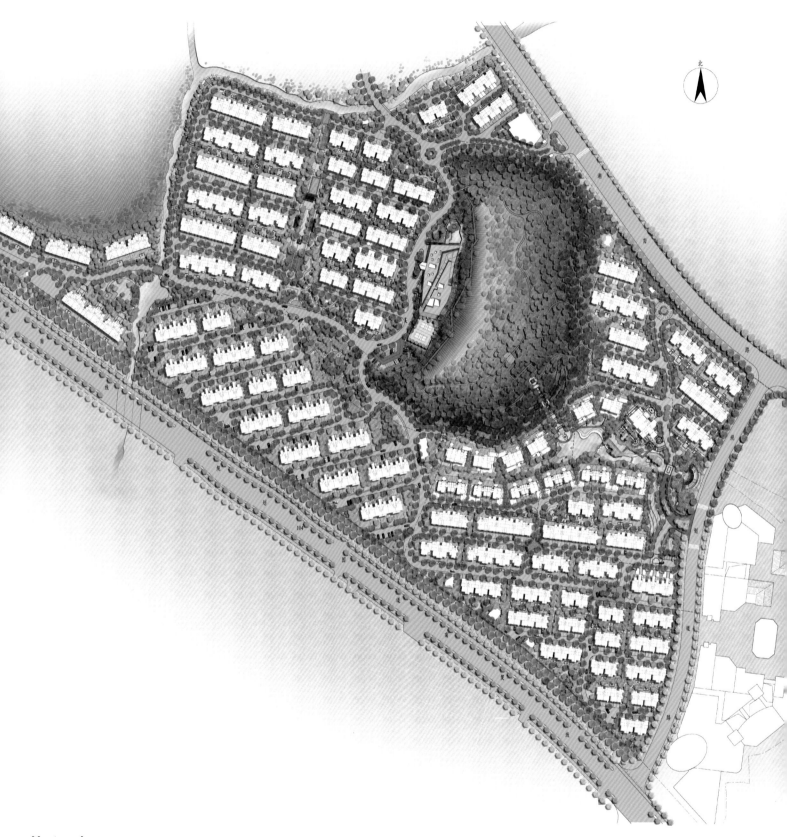

Master plan

1. Good inheritance to the architecture style
is fully shown in the landscape design
2-4. The pavement detail
5. The landscape furniture
6. The unique concept of "Hidden Mountain –
Rock Spa Resort Town"

7. The path with green plants
8. The wandering and quiet path
9. The wall with lush green plants
10. The project selects several species of local herbs to introduce a "fitness" concept
11. The stairs

With "Ecological Fitness" as its essence, the project selects several species of local herbs to introduce a "fitness" concept. By the configuration of herbs, fitness paths (i.e. the jogging loop which also functions as bicycle lane around main road of the living park) and mountainous landscape of fitness and leisure space carries out the "fitness" concept through the project. The humanised design reflects humanistic care and returns to the origin of fitness living.

VANKE VEGA BAY VILLAS, SHENZHEN

Location: Shenzhen, China
Completion: 2011
Design: Line and Space,LLC, SED Landscape Architects Co.,LTD.
Photography: SED Landscape Architects Co.,LTD.
Area: 300,000sqm

Located in the resort of Shenzhen Gold Coast, between Dameisha and Xiaomeisha, Tianqin Bay villa development enjoys an excellent ocean view and luxurious supporting facilities. For this villa development in South China which boasts best of its kind in South China, "Ocean View" is its greatest landscape advantage. The landscape designers highlight the development's identity and uniqueness through this scarce resource. With the theme "Expressing noble heart and enjoying free life", the landscape design emphasises Tianqin Bay's market positioning and creates a seafront high-class villa development with harmonious landscape, unique architectural space, elegant community atmosphere and noble lifestyle. The design should both show the project's luxury to promote clients' identities and satisfy their pursuits of freedom and ocean feeling. The 48 villas each possess their individual territory, which integrate with surroundings appropriately, without any artificial feeling.

Owners who live in Tianqin Bay "see nothing but mountains, sea and sky; hear nothing but ocean billows, sound of wind and bird tweet; smell nothing but fragrance of flowers and fresh air". They "live in a retreat and enjoy bay life". The landscape designers use natural elements complemented with contemporary facilities to create a unique leisure living environment, where people enjoy sky of Miami, coast of Naples, coast road of Melbourne and resort of Hawaii without leaving home.

The site has a mountain topography, so enclosure walls are arranged in response to slope instead of in a broken line, which otherwise will increase construction difficulty. Mainly consist of clean columns and wrought iron, the walls are simple styled and smartly hidden in the environment. With walls closely integrated in natural environment, the design ensures owner's security without cutting the internal and external environment. The designers use light overhangs and minimise the use of retaining walls, which protects natural topography and planting to a maximum level. The landscape design aims to achieve a balance between the development and environment. Since the discrepancy in elevation is nearly 70 metres, vertical site landscape design becomes the focus of the work.

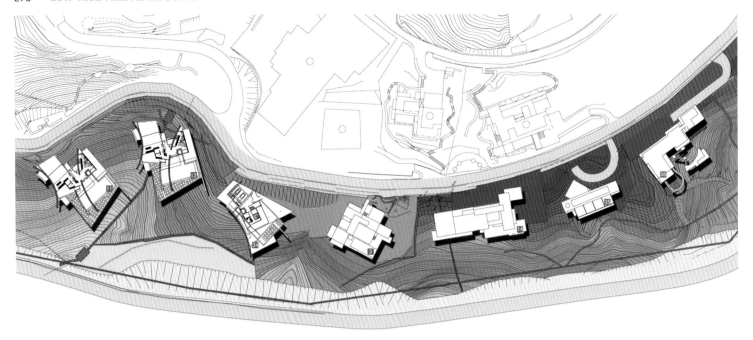

1. The site has a mountain topography
2. The path with green plants
3. Enclosure walls are arranged in response to slope instead of
in a broken line
4-6. Natural elements are complemented with contemporary
facilities to create a unique leisure living environment

7. Live in a retreat and enjoy bay life
8. The pavilion
9. Mainly consist of clean columns and wrought iron, the walls are simple styled and smartly hidden in the environment
10. Exterior space for relaxing and enjoying the sea

TANG ISLAND, SUZHOU

Location: Suzhou, China
Completion: 2012
Design: Tsutomu Yoshizawa (Yoshiki Toda Landscape & Architect Co.,Ltd.)
Photography: Yanlord Land Co., Ltd.
Client: Yanlord Land Co., Ltd.
Area: 53,800sqm

Located in a small island, the project takes broad Dushu Lake as its background. The landscape design aims to explore every features of the project and create an excellent housing environment. In the designers' interpretation, an excellent housing environment is: Sediment from Su Zhou's tradition and culture; Detachment from openness of a resort-like environment; Comfort from rich natural elements; Lifestyle from request of quality; Maturity from witness of time; Simplicity from pursuit of Zen.

To achieve this aim, the designers have taken following methods: first, they developed a detailed subdivided environment to make the project last with time; second, they created a home-returning experience with rich plots.

The former is a calm and relaxing space. Common landscape elements such as water and forest contrast with modern buildings, while they complement each other as well. A meandering creek runs through the whole site. Along our feet, stone paving and features with abundant plantings ease our heart. Although these landscape elements are common, the designers accent them with modern elements, providing the space rhythms and dynamics. Meanwhile, the Chinese traditional themes of "Plum, Orchid, Bamboo and Chrysanthemum" express a transition from urban environment to suburban environment. The latter is expressed in multi-layered home-entry experience: people travel through various custom designed entrances, go across delicate bridges, confront with terraced water features and pass through shades of tree canopies to return their homes.

1. People comes to the bridge following the sound of water guegling of the water fall

2. Concise and modern door scene
3. The succinct bridge design
4. The rhythmical stone pavement of the bridge, showing respect to the culture and tradition of Suzhou
5. The water feature on the two sides of the bridge

1. Water deck
2. Pavilion
3. South island
4. Parking apron
5. Barbecue deck
6. Connecting bridge
7. Pedestrian bridge
8. Garden swimming pool
9. Wooden bridge walkway
10. Reflection pool
11. Connecting bridge
12. Terraced deck
13. Yacht marina
14. Trickle

15. Entrance bridge of individual villa
16. Water ambulatory
17. Bank stone deck
18. Sundeck of individual villa
19. Island
20. Entrance vehicular bridge of individual villa
21. Club parking

22. Main entrance
23. Approach bridge
24. Cascading water feature
25. Wild bird conservation zone

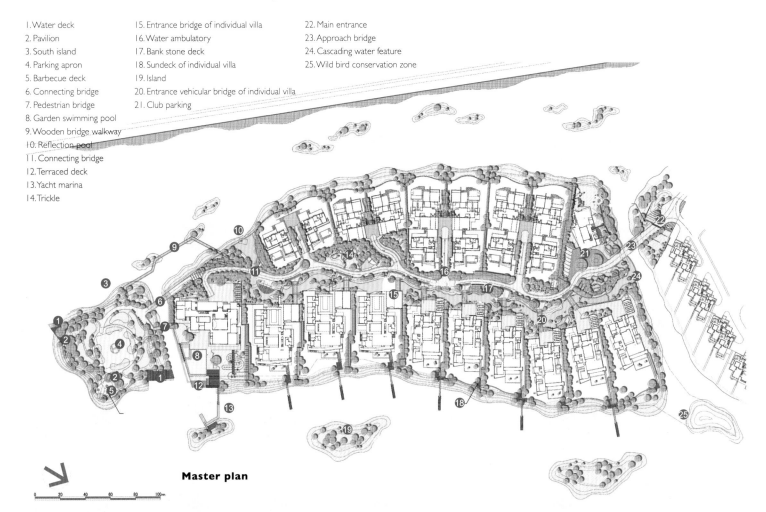

Master plan

0   20   40   60   80   100m

6. The concise pond at the entrance which shows the contemporary architecture
7. The path changes wonderingly and slowly
8. The atrium embodies the zen mood
9. Covered deck chair, which is comfortable and relaxing; the connection of stone and wood deck reflects contemporary style

8

9

The designers configured large amount of water and stone features in living space to respond to the traditions of Su Zhou, a famous watery town. These design elements not only express the respect to culture and tradition, but also enhance the intimacy of housing and highlight the owner's dignity.

Indulged in this natural, quiet and comfortable environment, with the footprints of time, your lifestyle will tend to real beauty and purity.

Index

C.F. Møller Architects
http://www.cfmoller.com

ONG&ONG Pte Ltd
http://ong-ong.com

ICN Design International Pte Ltd.
http://www.icn-design.com.sg

Tierra Design (S) Pte Ltd
http://www.tierradesign.com.sg

Espace Libre
http://www.espace-libre.fr

EARTHSCAPE
http://www.earthscape.co.jp

HASSEL
http://hassellstudio.com

Horizon & Atmosphere Landscape Co.
http://www.hsland.com.tw

SED Landscape Architects Co.,LTD.
http://www.sedgroup.com

One Landscape Design Limited
http://www.one-landscape.com

wa-so design
http://www. wa-so.jp

Taylor Cullity Lethlean
http://www.tcl.net.au

Williams Asselin Ackaoui & Associates Inc
http://waa-ap.com

Line and Space,LLC, SED Landscape Architects Co.,LTD.
http://www.lineandspace.com

© 2015 by Design Media Publishing Limited
This edition published in June 2015

Design Media Publishing Limited
20/F Manulife Tower
169 Electric Rd, North Point
Hong Kong
Tel: 00852-28672587
Fax: 00852-25050411
E-mail: suisusie@gmail.com
www.designmediahk.com

Editing: Viraj Chatterjee
Proofreading: Catherine Chang
Design/Layout: Zhou Jie

ISBN 978-988-12968-8-7

Printed in China